Jason Roberts

Born in New Zealand, Jason Roberts grew up in Brooweena, Queensland, where he loved growing watermelons and zucchinis in the chook pen, catching yabbies in the dam and selling mushrooms at the local shop for 30 cents a bag.

At 18, he began an apprenticeship at Ravesi's in Bondi, Sydney, where he quickly excelled and in 1993 was awarded 'Apprentice of the Year' by East Sydney Technical College. Roberts developed a love for French cooking at Armstrong's in Manly, and then accepted a position at Bistro Moncur, where he spent four and a half years as head chef.

Roberts now hosts the Nine Network's cooking program, *Fresh*, which screens every weekday Australia-wide and twice a day in New Zealand. He is an extremely active person and likes to spend his spare time surfing, dancing, indoor rock climbing and going to the gym.

jason roberts

graze

lots of little meals fast

MACMILLAN
Pan Macmillan Australia

First published 2003 in Macmillan by Pan Macmillan
Australia Pty Limited
St Martins Tower, 31 Market Street, Sydney

National Library of Australia
cataloguing-in-publication data:

Roberts, Jason, 1974– .
Graze: lots of little meals fast.

ISBN 0 7329 1174 5

1. Quick and easy cookery. I. Title

641.555

Designed and typeset by Naomi Simpson and Seymour Designs
Styled by Kylie Jaye
Photography by Simon Davidson
Printed by Imago Productions (F.E.) Pte. Ltd.

Contents

FROM LEFT: My mum Sharon, my partner Kylie, my nana Magda and me, Easter 2002.

"Nana, I want to be a Cook!"

That was you Jason, twenty-four years ago 'helping me' in the kitchen - you were just four years old - all cute and curly-haired! I never dreamt that simple statement would become your future....

Perhaps cooking is simply in your genes; Grandad and I earned our living catering and Nana Dawn ran her busy restaurant.

You loved camping out with your friends building campfires and cooking fresh-caught yabbies from the dam. You mastered the wood stove and made damper bread for everyone - you just love to cook!

When the microwave oven arrived you made 'cooked peanut-butter sandwiches' and learned how not to explode eggs!!

Despite your many other interests you always remained insistent you would be a Chef.

At just eighteen you accepted your apprenticeship and made me (all of us) so proud of your commitment. That seems like just yesterday.

Now, here I am in my 80s and I am thrilled, we still share our lunchtimes in the kitchen...
...Only things are a little different
...you now Entertain me!

I watch you even more than Oprah!
Good luck with this book - your first book.
Your biggest fan
Nana xxx

P.S I was so pleased you used my rissolia and rissoles.

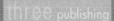

A cookbook is never just about recipes. I received an immeasurable amount of assistance from some very special people without whom this book would not have been possible. Now that the dust has settled (or in our case, the flour), I realise this book took nine cooking days (15-hour, 15-meal days), 50 loads of dishwashing, a dozen Shopfast deliveries, a few hundred dishes and a whole lot of sweat. My special thanks to:

Alison Adams – My amazing 'right-hand chick' in the kitchen. Al, thanks for prepping and scrubbing and testing, testing – one, two, three! You are amazing, talented and a bloody great cook.

Simon Davidson – The man with an eye for a shot – or 500! Your ability to capture the essence of these dishes (and eat most of them) has made me really excited. You're incredibly talented and a half-decent bloke!
Simon Davidson Photography: simondavidson@iprimus.com.au

Rob Fitzpatrick and David Woodward at Shopfast – The dynamic duo! Thanks for your belief and interest in this book and for that delivery of food every cooking day. Shopfast is such a great service – how did I ever live without you?
Shopfast: www.shopfast.com.au

Malcolm Pillage and Gary Horwitz at Bayswiss – Each time I enter one of your amazing stores I leave broke. I want one of everything. I am honoured that you let us use your crockery, décor, mats, platters and perfect products to style our dishes.
Bayswiss: www.bayswiss.com.au

Bernadette Foley, Tracey Cheetham and Brianne Tunnicliffe at Pan Macmillan – A huge thanks to my publishers for believing in, editing, advising, promoting and yes, selling, our book. Thank you for holding our hands and being my 'chef's shoulder'.
Pan Macmillan: www.panmacmillan.com.au

Naomi Simpson and the team at onetosix's 'three publishing' division – Thanks for everything. You guys made my thoughts and dreams a living, tangible reality. Naomi (Mummy no.1), you really rock!

Kylie Jaye – My creative director and stylish stylist. Despite having to work with my horrible schedule, your eye for texture, colour and detail in every dish was as dynamic as your overall vision for the book.
onetosix: kylie@onetosix.biz

Jason can be contacted through his management: Jasonroberts@satelliteagency.com

Kylie Jaye, my peaceful princess. Without you there would be no book. Thank you for making a dream a reality. Not only did you write, clean, style, host and inspire, you held me together through a hard year. With all my heart I love you and thank you for being so real. May this be the first of many more adventures to come. X

I'd also like to thank everyone I've ever had the opportunity of bumping shoulders with in a real kitchen. Each and every one of you has been an inspiration, especially you, DP and Tahlia. Thank you.

Introduction

I have wanted to cook for as long as I can remember. It's something I do to indulge my imagination, be creative, and feed my artistic passion. To me, cooking is the most consistent of life's joys and is immeasurably rewarding – instantly and constantly.

I've learnt a few things along the way, from running a restaurant where leisure, pleasure and indulgence were everything, to cooking healthy and nutritious dishes on television for families on a budget. The past few years have been a culinary challenge. They have given me a real understanding of people's need for alternatives – for a healthier, more varied diet, meals that can be planned and prepared regularly and easily, and meals where the enjoyment comes from cooking as well as eating. And I've found the best way to do all this is with lots of little meals.

I often have people ask me how I stay in relatively good shape when I am a chef. Believe me, I eat a lot of food. Lots. But the meals are little. Instead of the traditional three meals a day, I eat five or six small meals to keep my metabolism up. Eating small meals also means I get a wide variety of food, which is good for my health and my tastebuds!

This book contains a huge variety of smaller, delicious and healthy meals using staples you have at home like pasta, tomatoes, potatoes and rice, thrown together with other fresh veges, meat and poultry, eggs and fish.

It shows heaps of ways for you to make food tasty, different and interesting. The meals use readily available ingredients, and they're fast – you should have most of these recipes nailed in less than 20 minutes flat! If you are anything like me, you are probably juggling a million different responsibilities with work, family and social life. The last thing you need is a long, complicated recipe or an arduous marathon in the kitchen, so get stuck into these instead.

Graze is divided into sections for each of the nine basics I use (I've even colour-coded each section so you can easily find it again) and I've included some side dish options, some snacks (sassy snacks – who can live without them?) and yes, there's something for the sweet tooths too, with wicked smaller treats.

So get started – and let this book become your new best friend! Just whip up a couple of delectable dishes, relax and graze.

Enjoy!

Jason

Jason's spice cupboard

Here are some basic items you will need to stock so you are well prepared no matter what you want to cook.

Jase's top 10 'instant flavours'

SPICE	WHAT I USE IT FOR
black pepper and sea salt	I use them for just about everything and anything. They are an absolute necessity
chilli flakes	Pastas, stir-fries, vegetables, meats, Asian-style dishes
fennel seeds	Roasting, vegie dishes, risottos
nutmeg	Gnocchi, potato dishes, sweets
dried tarragon	Poaching chicken, lots of sauces
mixed herbs	Roasting, meats, barbecued dishes, sauces, breads
cinnamon quills	Sweets, curries, fruits (especially in poaching)
cloves	Pickling, desserts, curries
dried rosemary	Roasting, stews, pasta dishes, baked dishes
star anise	Sautéed prawns, seafood

Rice is an exceptionally versatile staple. As well as accompanying a wide variety of foods, rice can be a meal in itself and leftovers make great stir-fries.

Here's a rundown of the different varieties of rice and what they are used for.

LONG GRAIN WHITE Great for steaming, stir-fries and fried rice.

ARBORIO Risotto rice. Use it for any dish that you make from a risotto base (patties, arancini, etc).

BASMATI Fairly plain, long grain rice. Use it for curries and dishes with strong flavours.

JASMINE A long grain variety that is very fragrant and flavoursome, jasmine rice is often used for Thai dishes or as an accompaniment for curries or stir-fried dishes.

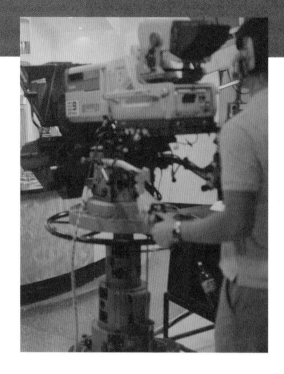

SHORT GRAIN Sushi rice. Used for sushi and other Japanese dishes. It looks a little like arborio rice when cooked – rounded and plump. You can tell it is done when it is tender while still maintaining its nutty texture.

MEDIUM GRAIN Used for rice pudding and other desserts. Its high starch content means it sticks together and offers a distinct creaminess when cooked. Great if a 'chewy' finish is desired, for a Thai rice egg pudding, for example.

rice

Basic cooked long or medium grain rice

I don't like to boil rice – I find it tends to lose its flavour in the litres of water. I prefer steaming it or using an absorption method, both of which maintain the nutty flavour and texture of the rice. If you eat a lot of rice, like I do, invest in a steamer. It will soon be your favourite kitchen appliance! If you don't have one, try this absorption method.

Jason's absorption method

If you want great, fluffy rice that's not sticky or gluggy, wash your rice before cooking (especially jasmine rice), then rinse it under cold water until the water runs clear. The methods below are for long and medium grain rice. Both will produce 3 cups of cooked rice.

1 cup rice, washed

2 cups water

a pinch salt

⊙ Place the washed rice, water and salt into a medium-sized saucepan.
⊙ Bring to the boil, then reduce the heat to very low and cover with a folded tea towel and then a lid.
⊙ Cook without stirring for 15 minutes, or until the liquid has been absorbed. Remove from the heat and fluff the rice with a fork. Cover and stand for 2 minutes.

Microwave method

⊙ Using the same basic ingredients, place the rice, salt and water into a medium-sized, microwave-proof bowl.
⊙ Cook on high, leaving uncovered, for 17 minutes. Remove and cover with a lid. Stand for 2 minutes before fluffing and serving.

Jase's 2 cents Wok tips

A wok will collect oils and food residues which become embedded in the surface coating, and make for better tasting cooking. This is referred to as 'wok seasoning'.

Never scrub your wok with a scourer or use harsh detergent, because they will remove the non-stick surface. Rub it with oil before putting it away.

Use a lightweight wok. You might see chefs using the big industrial ones, but there is no real advantage (except that they may last longer). The lightweight model will save you getting a sore wrist.

Electric woks are fabulous. They have very even heat distribution and are better than a basic wok if you don't have a gas stove.

stir-fried rice with asparagus
and oyster mushrooms

stir-fried rice with crab and chilli

Stir-fried rice with asparagus and oyster mushrooms

I love cooking with a wok. It's quick, easy, one-pot cooking – the bachelor's best friend! Serve and eat this one straightaway. Asparagus doesn't freeze or refrigerate very well, and the sauce will make the food a bit soggy over time. Serves 2.

1 cup cooked long grain rice
  (see page 6)
1 tablespoon vegetable oil
1 clove garlic, finely sliced
1/2 teaspoon chilli flakes
2 green shallots, finely sliced
2 spears asparagus, finely sliced
1 small handful oyster mushrooms
1/4 cup frozen peas
1 tablespoon soy sauce
1 teaspoon sesame oil
1 teaspoon sweet soy sauce
fresh chilli, thinly sliced

⊙ Cook the long grain rice and set it aside.
⊙ In a wok or thick-based frying pan, heat the oil till it starts to smoke. Add the garlic, chilli and shallots and fry, constantly moving them around with a wok spoon so they don't burn, till the ingredients are golden in colour.
⊙ Throw in the asparagus and oyster mushrooms and continue to stir-fry for a further 30 seconds.
⊙ Add the soy sauce, sesame oil and sweet soy sauce followed by the cooked rice and frozen peas, and heat for 5–7 minutes, or until all ingredients are cooked through. Garnish with the chilli and serve.

NOTE: Sweet soy is quite thick and viscous in comparison to plain soy.

Stir-fried rice with crab and chilli

This is a fantastic recipe. I like to pile it high on an Asian-style flat plate to serve. Don't be put off by the fact that I use tinned crabmeat – it's cheap, easy to find and available all year round. Serves 2.

2 tablespoons light olive oil
2 cloves garlic, crushed
1 chilli, chopped
1 cup cooked long grain rice
  (see page 6)
170 g tinned crabmeat, well drained
1 teaspoon fish sauce
1 tablespoon oyster sauce
1 teaspoon brown sugar
a squeeze lemon juice
1 small handful bean sprouts
2 shallots, sliced
1/4 cup fresh basil leaves

⊙ Heat the oil in a wok. Swirl to coat the wok with oil. When the oil begins to smoke, add the garlic and chilli and stir-fry for 30 seconds. Add the cooked rice and crabmeat and stir-fry until the rice has warmed through.
⊙ In a bowl, mix together the fish and oyster sauces, the sugar and lemon juice. Add this mixture to the wok, along with the bean sprouts, shallots and basil. Toss through until all ingredients are evenly mixed and serve.

Chicken and mushroom pilaf

This is a great, one-pot, light dish not unlike a baked risotto. Serve the leftovers cold with a salad or take to work for lunch and heat in the microwave. Serves 2.

1 tablespoon olive oil
2 chicken thigh fillets, cut into chunks
1 onion, chopped
1 clove garlic, crushed
100 g Swiss brown mushrooms, sliced
1 cup uncooked long grain rice, washed (try basmati or jasmine)
1³/4 cups chicken stock
1 bay leaf
1 tablespoon butter

⊙ Heat the oil in a saucepan. Brown the chicken, but do not cook it through, then set it aside. Add the onions to the pan and cook for 3 minutes, then add the garlic and Swiss brown mushrooms. Cook for a further 2 minutes.

⊙ Stir in the rice and return the chicken to the pan. Add the stock and the bay leaf and bring to the boil, then lower the heat and cover the saucepan with a tight-fitting lid. Simmer over low heat for 20 minutes (you don't have to stir it).

⊙ Remove the lid, stir in the butter and take the saucepan off the heat. Cover and stand for a further minute. Season with salt and pepper and serve.

Vegetable donburi

I do love my donburi! This dish is a bit of a cross between a stir-fry and a risotto – Asian style. It's not the prettiest dish, but it is pretty tasty. I like to serve it up in a small, deep bowl. Serves 2–4.

1 cup uncooked Japanese short grain rice
2 cups water
a pinch salt
1 tablespoon light olive oil
1 onion, cut into wedges
2 Japanese (slender) eggplants, cut into rounds
1 orange sweet potato, cubed (cubes should be about 2 cm x 2 cm)
2 tablespoons soy sauce
2 tablespoons mirin
1 tablespoon sugar
2 eggs

⊙ Rinse the rice well and place in a saucepan with the water and salt. Bring to the boil, cover and reduce the heat. Simmer for 20 minutes without stirring.

⊙ While the rice is cooking, heat the oil in a deep frying pan. Cook the onion, eggplant and sweet potato for 10 minutes or until browned.

⊙ Add the cooked rice, soy sauce, mirin and sugar to the vegetables, and cook for about 3 minutes, or until the rice has warmed through.

⊙ Beat the eggs in a small bowl. Pour them over the hot rice mixture and let it cook through, not stirring, for a couple of minutes.

⊙ Cover the pan and turn off the heat. Stand for 5 minutes, then serve.

NOTE: I use mirin (a Japanese rice wine), which adds a sweetness to counter the salty soy. It is available in Asian food shops and major supermarkets. If you don't have any, replace it with a teaspoon of sugar in ¹/4 cup white wine vinegar, or use 2 tablespoons of dry sherry.

vegetable donburi

Basic risotto

The thing I like about risotto is that once you have made the base, you can add just about anything to it. Sometimes I have a craving for that pure basic risotto taste, but armed with any meat or vegie and a few spices, it can be your most versatile dish.

Making risotto well in advance is okay too, and it can be helpful if you're planning a big dinner party. If you're making it the night before, cook the rice up to the point where you need to add the last third of the liquid, then store in an air-tight container or cover in cling wrap, and refrigerate. About 20 minutes before you want to serve it, add the remaining liquid and Parmesan, and cook until your risotto is hot all the way through and all the liquid has been absorbed. Risotto keeps very well in the fridge, and is not bad served cold. The basic recipe below serves 2.

1 tablespoon olive oil

2 tablespoons butter

1 onion, peeled and finely chopped

1 cup uncooked arborio rice

$1/2$ cup white wine

$2^{1}/_{2}$ cups stock or water, hot and salted (you should be able to taste the salt without it being too salty)

$1/4$ cup grated Parmesan cheese

⊙ Heat the oil and half the butter in a thick-based saucepan over moderate heat. Add the onions and cook till they are soft and translucent.

⊙ Add the rice and stir for about 30 seconds, or until the grains are glazed and translucent. Pour in the white wine and stir till it has been absorbed.

⊙ Lower the heat slightly and proceed to add the hot salted water a little at a time until all of it has been absorbed. This should take around 15–20 minutes. Then remove the saucepan from the heat.

⊙ Throw in the Parmesan and the remaining butter, and mix till they are evenly incorporated.

⊙ Have a taste. Give the risotto a good grinding of pepper and a small amount of salt, depending on your preference.

Jase's 2 cents
Stock tips (and I'm not talking about the Aussie dollar!)

Always use stock that is MSG free.

Should you make your own? Unless you're a commercial chef – who has the time? Tetra-pack liquid stock is great and there are some very good powdered stocks on the market now. They are widely available. If you do have the time, here's my recipe for quick and easy stock:

Jason's quick chicken stock

MAKES 4 CUPS

500 g chicken pieces (4–6 chicken legs)

1 tablespoon olive oil

1 teaspoon salt

a pinch pepper

5 cups water

Heat the olive oil in a medium-sized to large saucepan over high heat.

Brown the chicken legs, but do not cook them through. Add the salt and pepper, then cover with the water, making sure all the chicken is submerged.

Bring to the boil and simmer for about 20 minutes.

Strain the stock, then skim the excess fat from the top by scooping it out with a large serving spoon or ladle.

The stock can be frozen for later use – it lasts up to 2 months in an air-tight container.

Other risotto methods

While standing at the stove stirring risotto can be quite calming and therapeutic, often we're too pushed for time to make it the traditional way. Here are two easier ways to achieve a similar, creamy risotto texture.

Oven-baked risotto

Why oven bake? The answer is to save time and effort. Oven baking is great for those of us who want to be out of the kitchen while our food cooks (the 'lazy man's method', if you like). Use the same ingredients as a basic risotto (see page 12).

⊙ Preheat the oven to 180°C.

⊙ Heat the oil and half the butter in a thick-based ovenproof dish over medium heat. (If you choose an ovenproof dish with no plastic handles, etc, you can take it straight from the stove and put it in the oven later.)

⊙ Add the onion and cook, stirring, until soft. Add the rice and stir until the grains are translucent, then add the wine and continue stirring. When the wine has been absorbed, add all the salted water, bring to the boil and then cover with a tight-fitting lid.

⊙ Bake in the oven for 25 minutes or until the liquid has been absorbed and the rice is tender.

⊙ Remove from the oven, stir in the extra butter and Parmesan, and season with cracked pepper. If there is still some excess liquid, replace the lid and let stand for 5 minutes before serving.

Microwave risotto

I'm not a huge fan of using my microwave, but it's a mega timesaver in risotto emergencies! Once again, use the same basic ingredients (see page 12).

⊙ Place the oil, half the butter and the onion in a medium-sized, microwave-proof dish. Cook in the microwave on high for 2 minutes. Add the rice and cook for a further 30 seconds.

⊙ Add the wine and water and cook for about 10 minutes, or until half the liquid has been absorbed. Stir well and cook on high for a further 10 minutes.

⊙ Remove and test to see if the rice is tender. If not, microwave for a further few minutes. When cooked through, add the remaining butter and Parmesan and season with salt and pepper.

⊙ Stand, covered, for about 5 minutes, then serve.

Mussel and saffron risotto

Mussels are like miniature stock packages, releasing their salty flavour as they open during cooking. Serving them in their shells looks great, and the shells make for cool little scoops if you are in the mood for getting into your meal with your hands!

Some tips on mussels: never use a mussel if it is open before it is cooked, if it doesn't open when you cook it, or if it smells at all suspect. Choose the best, and the freshest, and they'll be delicious. Serves 2–4.

NOTE: *This recipe uses one quantity of basic risotto, but without the Parmesan (Italians traditionally don't put Parmesan in their seafood risottos).*

400 g black mussels

2 tablespoons olive oil

1/4 cup white wine

1 quantity basic risotto (see page 12), but incorporating the reserved mussel liquid into the 2 1/2 cups water or stock

a pinch saffron threads (or a pinch turmeric)

3 ripe tomatoes or 200 g crushed tomatoes, finely chopped

1 tablespoon light sour cream

2 tablespoons chopped parsley

Jase's 2 cents
My trip to hospital

An embarrassing occasion for me but take note: if you are cooking for guests, you may want to check if they are sensitive to seafood. Allergies to seafood, especially mussels or clams, are very common. The body will quickly tell you if you are allergic – it might be a rash, swelling of the throat or shortness of breath. A bad mussel can be serious, as I discovered the day we photographed this dish. The entire shoot team thought it was hilarious when I broke out in a rash from eating a few mussels before deciding they were not quite as fresh as they should have been. But the laughter quickly subsided when they discovered I was having trouble breathing!

⊙ Clean the mussels by scrubbing them quickly under cold running water and removing their 'beards' (these are the frilly, hairy-looking fringes of flesh between the two shells which are not edible).

⊙ Covered with a tight-fitting lid, heat the olive oil in a saucepan over medium to high heat. When the oil starts to smoke, add the mussels and white wine and replace the lid. Shake the pan gently over the heat, backwards and forwards, for about 30 seconds.

⊙ Keeping the pan on the heat, remove the lid and take out the mussels as they open. If any don't open, don't use them. When all have been removed, strain the remaining liquid and set it aside.

⊙ When the mussels have cooled, remove the flesh from about 2/3 of the shells and leave the remaining mussels intact for presentation.

⊙ Cook the risotto as per the basic recipe (see page 12), incorporating the reserved mussel liquid and pinch of saffron into the 2 1/2 cups of water or stock. (Don't salt the water till you have added the mussel stock, as mussel juice has a tendency to be salty.)

⊙ Once the rice has absorbed all of the liquid, stir in the tomatoes.

⊙ When you add the remaining butter, stir in the mussel flesh, along with the sour cream and chopped parsley. Top with the mussels still in their shells and serve.

NOTE: *Chefs call turmeric 'poor man's saffron' because it makes a reasonable substitute, but using it instead of saffron gives a slightly different taste.*

mussel and saffron risotto

roast pumpkin, basil and
fennel risotto

Roast pumpkin, basil and fennel risotto

Pumpkin is always there, any season, all seasons! I like to use butternut pumpkin for this recipe because it has fewer seeds to extract and is easier to handle when you are cutting it up. However, you could use any of the varieties available – butternut, Queensland blue (great when you are feeding a big crew as they're usually bigger than other varieties), and Japanese, which tends to be smaller than your average butternut. Serves 2.

1 quantity basic risotto (see page 12)
1/3 quantity pumpkin roasted with
   fennel seeds and chilli (see page 109)
1 bulb baby fennel, sliced paper thin
1 bunch basil (about 20 leaves)

⊙ Prepare your basic risotto to the point where all the water has been absorbed. Stir through the roasted pumpkin, baby fennel and basil.
⊙ Stir the Parmesan and remaining butter through, and season well with salt and pepper. Serve.

Minted broad bean and Feta risotto

This recipe is fantastic – it's sweet and full of texture, and not too time-consuming provided you're using frozen peas and beans. If you're not a fan of peeling broad beans you can substitute them for more peas – but I think they are worth the effort. The flavour is phenomenal. Serves 2.

1 cup frozen broad beans
1 quantity basic risotto (see page 12)
1/2 cup frozen peas, defrosted
a few fresh mint leaves, torn
1 handful fresh baby spinach,
   chopped
125 g soft Feta cheese, preferably
   sheep-milk Feta, crumbled
cracked black pepper

⊙ To prepare the broad beans, plunge them into boiling, salted water for about 3 minutes, then strain and refresh in cold water. Peel away the outer skin, reserving only the bright green bean.
⊙ Cook the risotto as per the basic recipe. After the water has been absorbed add the peas, followed by the butter and Parmesan.
⊙ Adjust the seasoning to your taste and fold in the broad beans along with the torn mint leaves, chopped spinach and the crumbled Feta.
⊙ Serve with a grinding of fresh black pepper and a scattering of small mint leaves over the top.

Fontina and rosemary risotto

Following the basic risotto recipe and throwing in the cheese at the last moment is so easy it's embarrassing – but that's all there is to it. Fontina is a beautiful cow's milk cheese from northern Italy. It has a delicate, nutty flavour with a hint of honey, and I absolutely love it. If you can't get a hold of Fontina, try Heidi Gruyère, a fantastic Australian cheese that lends itself nicely to this recipe. I serve this dish with a big green salad dressed in lemon juice vinaigrette and olive oil, and hand-torn crusty bread. Serves 2.

1 quantity basic risotto (see page 12)
80 g Fontina cheese, diced into 0.5 cm cubes
1 teaspoon rosemary, roughly chopped

⊙ Follow the basic risotto recipe (see page 12), throwing in the teaspoon of chopped rosemary with the onions.
⊙ Fold the Fontina cheese through just before serving.

Mushroom risotto

When mushrooms are in season, there's an abundance of varieties to choose from. Most supermarket chains carry everything from fresh shiitake and black fungi to chestnut mushrooms, which all provide magnificent texture and flavour to risotto. You could stick to one or two mushroom types, or use several different varieties in this recipe. Dried mushrooms add another dimension to your risotto, though you will need to submerge them in boiling water to soften them before cooking. Mushroom risotto is also great with strips of seared seasoned chicken, and topped with shredded fresh snow peas. Serves 2.

1 quantity basic risotto (see page 12)
1 clove garlic, finely chopped
250 g mixed mushrooms, chopped into bite-size pieces
2 tablespoons chopped parsley

⊙ Add the garlic to the onions as they are softening. Then add the mushrooms, and proceed as for the basic risotto recipe.
⊙ Throw in the chopped parsley just before serving.

Chorizo, spinach and chickpea risotto

A gutsy recipe to enthuse the meat eaters, this one has heaps of flavour, loads of texture and is deceptively filling. Chorizo is a delicious, spicy Spanish sausage that is quite readily available. If you can't find chorizo, substitute it with bacon and a pinch of paprika. Serves 2–4.

1 quantity basic risotto (see page 12)
1 chorizo sausage (180 g), skin removed and cut into 1 cm cubes
1 teaspoon olive oil
1/4 teaspoon dried chilli flakes
3 ripe tomatoes, cut into small cubes, or 200 g crushed tomatoes
300 g tinned chickpeas, drained
1/2 cup frozen peas, defrosted
1 handful baby spinach

⊙ In a thick-based saucepan, brown the cubed chorizo in the olive oil over medium to high heat till evenly coloured. Remove and drain on absorbent paper.
⊙ Proceed as for the basic risotto recipe, adding the dry chilli flakes along with the onion and cooking until the onion is soft and translucent. Throw in the tomatoes after the wine has been absorbed, and then continue adding the water or stock.
⊙ Finish the basic risotto, then fold the chickpeas, peas and spinach through and cook until the spinach has wilted. Season with salt and pepper and serve.

NOTE: If using dry chickpeas, use 1 cup, soak overnight in water, and drain before use.

Arancini

Arancini are fried risotto balls with a yummy cheesy inside and crispy, crunchy outside. I like to top them with tomato sauce and squish them in a bread roll, but they're also great served with salsa or over salad, and as finger food at barbecues. They keep well in the fridge for quick snacks. Makes 8–10 arancini.

1 quantity basic risotto, cold (see page 12)
2 eggs
1 cup breadcrumbs
200 g Mozzarella cheese
olive or canola oil

⊙ Lightly beat one of the eggs and add to the cold basic risotto. Mix well and roll the risotto into golf-ball sized balls.
⊙ Make an indentation in each with your thumb and push in a small cube of Mozzarella.
⊙ Beat the other egg. Lightly flour the arancini, then dip them in the beaten egg and roll in breadcrumbs.
⊙ Pour enough oil into a pan to come about 1 cm up the sides and heat. Fry the arancini in the oil, turning frequently to avoid burning, until crisp.

Polenta is cornmeal, and a staple in Italian cooking. Some people think it is very difficult to prepare or is something only chefs cook, but once you give it a go, you'll see it is ultra-simple! Many traditional recipes for polenta say to cook it, stirring, for up to an hour. With instant polenta available these days, why bother? Even if the packet doesn't say 'instant', a lot of polenta will cook in under 15 minutes. Just make sure you use a fine rather than coarse grain variety.

NOTE: polenta firms upon cooling. If possible, serve it immediately and spoon the rest into a greased baking tin. This can then be fried or grilled and served with a sauce or vegetables. Also, polenta holds a lot of heat, and bubbles like the mud pools of Rotorua! Use a high-sided pan to avoid being burnt.

polenta

Soft polenta

Polenta is a bit like mashed potato – a gorgeous comfort food. It's one of the nicest accompaniments to 'meat and gravy' dishes, so give it a try. The basic recipe below serves 4.

2¹/2 cups chicken stock or salted water

100 g fine or instant polenta

40 g butter

¹/3 cup grated Parmesan

pepper

- Bring the stock or water to the boil in a saucepan. Slowly whisk in the polenta.
- Reduce the heat to low and stir for 12–15 minutes, or until the polenta pulls away from the sides of the pan.
- Stir in the butter and Parmesan. Season with pepper and serve immediately.

Firm polenta

Firm polenta is the best sort to use when you want to grill it. To make it, use only 2 cups of stock or water in the above recipe.

Firm polenta with goat's cheese and roasted tomato sauce

You can use any cheese you like for this dish, but I think it tastes best with goat's cheese, Mozzarella and shaved Parmesan. I used an aged French goat's cheese called Chabichou for this shot – it's a particular favourite of mine because of its mild, 'earthy' flavour and firm texture. Serves 4.

1 quantity firm polenta (see above)

2 tablespoons olive oil

1 quantity roasted tomato sauce
  (see page 52), warmed

10 x 0.5 cm slices aged goat's cheese
  (or goat's curd or Feta)

extra virgin olive oil

- Make the firm polenta (see above), and pour it into a loaf or slice tin that has been lined with baking paper.
- Put aside to set (this shouldn't take longer than 30 minutes). When set, turn it out onto a chopping board and cut it into 0.5 cm slices, like thick sliced bread.
- Heat the olive oil in a frying pan over moderate heat.
- Add the polenta pieces and fry for 1–2 minutes on each side, or until golden.
- Place a good dollop of the warm roasted tomato sauce onto two plates, and top with the polenta and goat's cheese. Drizzle with the extra virgin olive oil and serve.

firm polenta with goat's cheese
and roasted tomato sauce

soft polenta with blue
cheese and spinach

Soft polenta with blue cheese and spinach

Looks a little messy, but it's a taste sensation! I adore great blue cheeses. They add an unmatchable tangy, sharp flavour to a dish. But my girlfriend hates blue cheese, so I make this dish with other soft, tasty cheeses as well. Her favourite options are Swiss cheese, Mozzarella and Gruyère. Serves 2.

1 quantity soft polenta (see page 22)
2 cups baby English spinach leaves
50 g blue cheese, crumbled
30 g butter (optional)
Parmesan, shaved

⊙ Make the soft polenta (see page 22).
⊙ Stir the spinach leaves into the cooked polenta and cook until they have wilted.
⊙ Place a good dollop of polenta in each bowl. Crumble the blue cheese evenly over the top and fold it through lightly. For a richer taste, fold through the butter, or leave it out for a less fattening option. Shave Parmesan generously over the top and serve.

Soft polenta with corn and Parmesan

This is a hearty polenta that is very tasty served with braised beef (see page 77) or lamb shanks (page 78). Serves 4 as an accompaniment.

1 quantity soft polenta (see page 22)
400 g corn kernels or 1 cup frozen
  corn, defrosted
Parmesan, shaved

⊙ Make the soft polenta (see page 22).
⊙ Stir the corn through the cooked soft polenta.
⊙ Place a large dollop of polenta into each bowl. Shave Parmesan generously over the top and serve.

NOTE: Defrost frozen corn by running cold water through it until soft.

Soft polenta with tomato sauce and beef sausages

The ultimate comfort food! I like to spread the sauce and sausages right across the polenta for an even distribution of flavour. For a twist, I replace the sausages with chicken, pork, spiced sausage or even lamb or veal pieces. Serves 2–4.

2 tablespoons olive oil
2 good quality thick beef sausages
1 quantity roasted tomato sauce
(see page 52)
1–2 teaspoons balsamic vinegar
(optional)
2 tablespoons chopped parsley
1 quantity soft polenta (see page 22)

- Heat the oil in a medium-sized frying pan and cook the sausages for about 8 minutes. Remove from the heat and cool for a few minutes.
- Remove any excess oil from the pan and add the tomato sauce and balsamic vinegar (if using). Simmer gently for 2–3 minutes.
- Cut the sausages into 3 or 4 slices on the diagonal, then return them to the pan.
- Add the chopped parsley. Warm through, season, and serve on the soft polenta.

Pan-fried firm polenta with grilled vegetables

Serves 2.

1 quantity firm polenta (see page 22)
1 zucchini, thinly sliced lengthwise
2 Roma tomatoes, halved
6 spears thin asparagus, trimmed
200 g button mushrooms
2 tablespoons olive oil
1–2 tablespoons pesto

- Make the firm polenta (see page 22), and pour it into a loaf or slice tin that is greased or lined with baking paper.
- Put aside to set (this shouldn't take longer than 30 minutes). When set, turn it out onto a chopping board and cut into 14–16 slices, like thick sliced bread, and then into triangles if desired.
- In a bowl, toss the zucchini, tomatoes, asparagus and mushrooms with olive oil and season well with salt and pepper.
- Heat a chargrill plate or barbecue, making sure it is very hot before beginning. Cook the vegetables on both sides until soft and charred. Set them aside and then grill the polenta triangles until they are crisp. (It's also fine to pan-fry them slightly.)
- Place the polenta on plates and top with the vegetables. Drizzle with pesto, to taste. Serve.

Jase's 2 cents Grills

- Rub your grill with olive oil before cooking. Never clean a grill with a harsh scourer or detergent, as the build-up of oils on the surface will be altered. Clean it with hot water without detergent and wipe clean with a sponge or cloth.
- Grills need to be really hot before adding anything, especially vegies. Food will stick badly if the surface is not hot enough.

When I was a kid, there were only two types of potatoes – dirty and washed. These days the choice can seem overwhelming, so here are a few tips on the different varieties and how to store them. I keep my potatoes in the pots and pans cupboard because it is cool, dark and dry. If any moisture gets into your potatoes, they will start the germination process – the whole 'potato-has-eyes' thing.

Because everyone loves the taste of nutrient-rich potatoes, it's easy to prepare a healthy breakfast, lunch or dinner that both adults and kids will eat. Potatoes are full of energy-providing carbohydrates, and they don't contain any fat (until you add butter!). One medium-sized potato provides 45 per cent of the recommended daily intake of vitamin C, 21 per cent of the recommended daily intake of potassium, 3 grams of fibre and has only 100 calories.

DESIREE Available everywhere all year round. This type is very starchy and therefore makes the creamiest, most delicious mash.

KIPFLER Has a waxy, smooth skin. Perfect for slicing for salads, potato bake or chips.

SEBAGO The high starch content of this variety makes for the best, lightest and fluffiest chips and wedges.

CHATS Little taters! Whether boiled, baked or fried, these are a great accompaniment for meat dishes. Also make great potato salad.

COLIBAN Your average staple potato. I like to use these for chips because they are always in the shops, and already washed.

potatoes

Basic mashed potato

There's no denying it, the nicest mash is the one with the most butter! Feel free to substitute the milk with cream, if you're feeling decadent. Serves 2–4 as an accompaniment.

4 large potatoes, peeled and cut into
  chunks (I try to use Desiree
  potatoes)
50 g butter, roughly cubed
3/4 cup warmed milk or cream
salt, and black or white cracked
  pepper
a pinch nutmeg

○ Place the potatoes in a saucepan of cold water. Bring to the boil and cook for about 20 minutes or until tender.
○ Drain and return to the saucepan. Shaking the pan, cook for about 20 seconds to remove any excess moisture.
○ Remove the pan from the heat and mash the potatoes with a masher until smooth. You could also push the potato through a mouli or ricer into a bowl.
○ For a smooth mash, beat in the butter and milk until smooth and emulsified. Use a masher for a chunkier finish.
○ Season with the salt, white or black cracked pepper and nutmeg and serve.

NOTE: A ricer is a device that looks like a big garlic crusher – it pushes the mixture through little holes to form rice-sized 'grains'.

Crushed potatoes

This is a slightly healthier version of mash, because while olive oil has the same amount of fat as butter, it's a better fat for you as it is mono-unsaturated. I like leaving the skins on for a chewy, more textured mashed or crushed potato. Serves 2–4 as an accompaniment.

4 large potatoes (I try to use Desiree
  potatoes)
3 tablespoons olive oil

○ Place the potatoes in a saucepan of cold water. Bring to the boil and cook for 20 minutes.
○ Drain and return the potatoes to the saucepan. Mash them lightly with a fork (using a fork leaves nice chunky pieces of potato), adding olive oil as you go.
○ Season with salt and pepper and serve.

oven-baked potato croquettes

Bubble and squeak

There are as many recipes for bubble and squeak as there are grandmothers, which means that pretty much anything goes! The mash just acts as a binding agent. Mix all your ingredients together and either fry them up or make burger patties and serve them on a bread roll with crisp salad and tomato sauce. Serves 2.

1 cup leftover mashed potato

6 thick slices of roast beef or lamb, cut into small pieces

¼ cup frozen peas

1 onion, finely chopped

2 tablespoons chopped parsley

2 tablespoons olive oil

NOTE: You could also use 1 cup of cooked mince or a shop-bought whole roast chicken instead of the beef or lamb. For a vegetarian option use a mixed selection of fresh or frozen cooked vegetables.

⊙ Combine the mash, roast, peas, onion and parsley in a bowl.

⊙ Heat the oil in a frying pan, then add the mixture so that it is evenly spread over the pan, like a pancake. Cook for 1–2 minutes on each side, pressing with a spatula until cooked.

⊙ Serve with last night's leftover gravy or with bacon for brekky.

Oven-baked potato croquettes

Shop-bought croquettes don't come close to these babies – they are positively addictive! Makes 6 large or 12 small croquettes.

1 quantity mashed potatoes (see page 30)

1 egg yolk

2 whole eggs

⅓ cup dried breadcrumbs

2 tablespoons grated Parmesan

1 teaspoon dried mixed herbs (parsley, rosemary, salt and pepper work well)

olive oil spray

⊙ Preheat the oven to 200°C.

⊙ Mix the mash with the egg yolk. Roll into croquettes. Each should be an oval ball using about 2 tablespoons of mash. Use a teaspoon for smaller croquettes.

⊙ In a separate bowl, beat the whole eggs lightly with a fork. Season with salt and pepper.

⊙ In another bowl, combine the breadcrumbs, Parmesan and herbs.

⊙ Dip the croquettes in the beaten egg, then roll them in the breadcrumb mixture.

⊙ Place the croquettes on a baking tray and then spray lightly with the olive oil spray. Bake for 20 minutes until crisp and browned.

Whole baked jacket potatoes

A whole jacket potato has almost no fat (until you add it). For a perfect feast, I like to throw dips on my jacket potatoes – hummus, pesto, baba ghannouj, tahini or guacamole. Makes 2 baked potatoes.

2 large Sebago potatoes, unpeeled
1 tablespoon olive oil
1/3 cup ricotta
2 tablespoons grated Parmesan
1 tomato, diced
1 1/2 tablespoons olive paste or
  roughly chopped pitted olives

Preheat the oven to 200°C.
Prick the potatoes all over with a skewer. Rub them lightly with oil and place them directly on the top shelf of the oven. Roast for about an hour, or until the potatoes are tender.
Remove the potatoes from the oven and let them cool for a few minutes. Then slice the top off each potato and scoop out most of the flesh. Combine the flesh with the ricotta, Parmesan and tomato. Carefully place the mixture back into the potato and bake for a further 10 minutes or until the mixture bubbles. Top with the olive paste or olives and serve.

Baked potato chips

In the eighties everyone was proud to have their very own deep fryer, but these days we are all a little more heath conscious. I heard once that one deep-fried french fry had the same fat content as 8 baked jacket potatoes. That's enough to make anyone think twice if they have the option of baking instead! Serves 2.

2 large Sebago potatoes, cut into
  wedges
1 tablespoon olive oil
6 cloves garlic, still in their skin
1/2 tablespoon of dried rosemary
  (or a couple of sprigs of fresh)
1–2 tablespoons sea salt

Preheat the oven to 200°C.
In a bowl, toss the potato wedges with the oil, garlic and rosemary. Transfer to a baking dish and sprinkle with sea salt. Bake in the oven for about 40 minutes, shaking the pan occasionally, until the wedges are crisp and tender.

whole baked jacket potatoes

Chicken, green bean and potato salad

To peel Kipfler potatoes and other waxy varieties, simply steam or boil them until tender and then rub off the skin with your fingers while they're still warm. If the potato is not waxy (like a Desiree), peel it with a potato peeler before cooking. Serves 2.

4 medium-sized Kipfler or pink-eyed
  potatoes (200 g), scrubbed
1 cup baby beans (100 g), trimmed
1 tablespoon lemon juice
1 teaspoon grated lemon zest
2 tablespoons extra virgin olive oil
1½ tablespoons capers, rinsed and
  roughly chopped
1 poached tarragon chicken breast
  (see page 63), cut into 1–1.5 cm
  slices
1 tablespoon chervil sprigs (or
  parsley if you don't have chervil)

○ Place the potatoes in a saucepan of cold water. Bring to the boil and cook till tender right through (use a fork to test them). Remove the potatoes with a slotted spoon, cool for a few minutes, then peel and cut into 1 cm slices.
○ Place the beans into the boiling water. Cook for 3 minutes and drain.
○ To make the dressing, combine the lemon juice, lemon zest and olive oil in a small bowl.
○ Place the potatoes, beans, capers, chicken and chervil or parsley in a bowl. Season with salt and pepper and toss the dressing through. Serve.

Mustard potatoes

You can serve this delicious dish as an accompaniment to meats and fish (use the chats as a bed under a great slab of salmon – see page 90), or add them to a summer salad of lettuce, tomatoes, cheese and green beans. Serves 4.

8 chat potatoes

For the dressing:
1 heaped tablespoon seeded mustard
juice of half a lemon
3 tablespoons extra virgin olive oil
salt and pepper to taste

○ Place the potatoes in a pot of cold water. Bring to the boil and then remove the pot from the heat when the potatoes are soft but still a little firm. Cool for a few minutes, then halve the potatoes, leaving the skins on.
○ Combine the dressing ingredients and toss through the potatoes.

Potato gnocchi with zucchini and tomatoes

Fresh, shop-bought gnocchi is delicious, but it is so satisfying and impressive to make it yourself. This gnocchi is one of those dishes your friends will envy, but it's actually amazingly easy. I like to serve it with more vegetables than gnocchi.

NOTE: Uncooked gnocchi can be frozen. Freeze in batches and when you want to cook them, defrost and throw into boiling water.

For the gnocchi:

6 medium-sized Desiree potatoes
  (500 g), unpeeled
1 cup plain flour
30 g butter
1½ teaspoons salt
pepper to taste
¼ teaspoon nutmeg
¼ cup grated Parmesan

For the sauce:

⅓ cup extra virgin olive oil
2 cloves garlic, sliced
2 chillies, chopped
3 zucchinis, chopped
6 tomatoes, peeled, deseeded and
  chopped
2 tablespoons small basil leaves
Parmesan to serve

For the gnocchi:

◉ Place the potatoes in a steamer over simmering water. Cover and cook for 15 minutes or until just tender. Cool for a few minutes and push through a mouli or ricer. Alternatively, you can peel them before cooking and mash them afterwards.

◉ Gradually add the flour and mix to a dough-like consistency. You may need to use more or less flour depending on how wet the potatoes are. Add the butter, salt, pepper, nutmeg and Parmesan and knead gently (be careful not to overwork the dough or you will end up with tough, dense gnocchi).

◉ Divide the dough into 6 pieces. Roll each piece into cylinders about 2 cm thick and about 40 cm long. Cut these into 1.5 cm 'pillows'.

◉ Bring a large pot of salted water to the boil. Cook the gnocchi in batches until they float to the surface. This should take less than a minute.

For the sauce:

◉ Heat the oil in a large frying pan, then add the garlic and fry for 1 minute. Add the chilli and zucchini. Cook for a further 2 minutes. Add the tomatoes and season well with salt and pepper.

◉ Toss the sauce through the cooked gnocchi and serve scattered with basil leaves and shaved Parmesan.

Pasta is a great source of carbohydrate and provides sustained energy. It comes in a huge variety of shapes and sizes and takes varying amounts of time to cook. Different shapes hold different sauce types better than others, but feel free to mix'n'match the base and the topping, and see what combinations you like. Thin, delicate pastas like angel hair or thin spaghetti are wonderful served with light, delicate sauces. Thicker pasta shapes, like fettuccine, and those with holes or ridges, like mostacciolo or radiatore, are perfect with heavier, chunkier sauces. Virtually all pasta is delicious in soups, salads and stir-fries. Have fun and use whatever you have in your cupboard!

pasta

Here's my low-down on the various types

ALPHABET This shape is a kids' favourite, and is often used in soups for a fun meal any time.

ANGEL HAIR (CAPELLINI) Thin, delicate strands usually combined with lighter sauces.

CONCHIGLIE This shell-shaped pasta makes a great base for pasta salad, or as a substitute for macaroni in macaroni cheese.

DITALINI This pasta is shaped like little thimbles, from which it gets its name. This versatile shape can be used as the base of any dish.

FARFALLE This pasta is also known as bow-ties or butterflies.

FETTUCCINE This ribbon-like pasta is perfect for heavier sauces such as cheese, meat and tomato sauces.

FUSILLI This long, spiral-shaped pasta can be topped with any sauce and bakes particularly well in casseroles.

JUMBO SHELLS These are fantastic stuffed with mince flavoured with taco seasoning, topped with salsa and baked.

LASAGNE The name of this pasta comes from the Latin word for pot, *lasanum*. Make lasagne casseroles by using chopped vegetables, cheeses and any kind of sauce. You can also assemble your lasagne and freeze it for later.

LINGUINE These 'little tongues' are a great shape for all sauces.

MACARONI This highly versatile shape can be topped with any sauce and used in virtually any dish.

MANICOTTI This pipe-shaped pasta is lovely stuffed with a mixture of meat, cheese and vegetables, topped with your favourite sauce, and baked. Or, stuff and freeze for later.

ORZO This small, grain-shaped pasta can be topped with any sauce, added to soups, or baked in a casserole. It is perfect as a side dish as well as a main course.

PENNE, MOSTACCIOLI Meaning 'quills' and 'small moustaches' respectively, this tubular pasta goes well with most sauces.

RADIATORE The ruffled, ridged shape of this pasta goes well with any sauce, soup or salad.

RIGATONI The ridges and holes in rigatoni are perfect with chunky cream, cheese or meat-based sauces.

ROTINI The spiralled, twisted shape of rotini holds bits of meat, vegetables and cheese, so it works well with chunky sauces.

RUOTE These wagon wheels make interesting salads, casseroles and stir-fry dishes. Add them to soups, or simply top with a chunky sauce.

SPAGHETTI America's favourite pasta shape, spaghetti is the perfect choice for nearly any sauce, though it is wonderful with light sauces.

VERMICELLI Slightly thinner than spaghetti, these 'little worms' are great in stir-fries and broths.

ZITI A medium-sized, tubular pasta shape, ziti is beautiful with chunky sauces and meat dishes.

linguine with blue-eye
and vongole

Linguini with blue-eye and vongole

Despite its reputation, blue-eye is not a cod – it's a travella. You could actually use any tasty, firm white fish for this one. Vongole are clams and are superb in this dish; however, you can use mussels instead if you like. Serves 2.

200 g linguine
1/2 cup olive oil
3 cloves garlic, chopped
1/4 teaspoon chilli flakes or 2 bird's eye chillies, chopped
3 tablespoons parsley, finely chopped
200 g blue-eye, cut into 3 cm chunks
1/4 cup white wine
20 vongole (about 400 g)

⊙ Bring a large saucepan of salted water to the boil. Cook the linguine according to the instructions on the packet. Drain and set aside.

⊙ Heat the oil in a large, thick-based frying pan. Add the garlic, chilli and parsley and cook on medium heat for about 30 seconds. Add the blue-eye and cook, turning to avoid them sticking, for about 2 minutes.

⊙ Add the wine and vongole. Place the lid on the frying pan and cook, shaking the pan occasionally, until the vongole open. This should take 2–3 minutes.

⊙ Toss the linguine with the vongole mixture until warmed through. Season with salt and pepper and serve.

Fettuccine with broccoli, anchovy and chilli

Doesn't look half as good as it tastes, but it's jam-packed with goodness. The real bonus is that it's the kind of dish you can make with stuff you have in the cupboard already. Serves 2–4.

NOTE: The broccoli is supposed to be a little 'mushy', not firm as if steamed. This makes for a more consistently smooth texture through the dish.

1 head broccoli (125 g), broken into small florets
200 g fettuccine
1/3 cup olive oil
5 anchovy fillets, finely chopped
2 cloves garlic, finely chopped
1/4 teaspoon chilli flakes
1 tablespoon chopped parsley
1/4 cup Parmesan, grated or shaved
pepper

⊙ Bring a large saucepan of salted water to the boil. Add the broccoli and cook for about 5 minutes until tender. Remove with a slotted spoon and set aside. Add the fettuccine to the water and cook according to the instructions on the packet.

⊙ Heat the oil in a large frying pan, then add the anchovies and cook for a couple of minutes until they break down and start to look like a paste. Add the garlic and chilli and cook for a further 30 seconds. Now add the broccoli and cook, stirring, for about 2 minutes, or until the broccoli begins to become soft and fall apart.

⊙ Drain the pasta and toss it through the broccoli mixture, along with the parsley and Parmesan. Season with pepper and serve.

Orecchiette with minted lentils and Feta

Orecchiette is a small 'ear' shaped pasta. Any short pasta can be used (eg, shells, twists or penne), but I like this as it holds the lentils inside it like a mini-cup. Serves 4.

100 g green beans

150 g orecchiette

1/4 cup olive oil

2 cloves garlic, chopped

400 g tinned brown lentils, drained
  and rinsed

2 tablespoons chopped mint

1 1/2 tablespoons balsamic vinegar

1 small Spanish onion, sliced

1/3 cup basil leaves, torn

150 g marinated Feta, crumbled

⊙ Bring a large saucepan of salted water to the boil. Add the beans and cook for 3 minutes. Remove with a slotted spoon and set aside. Cut the beans into thirds. Add the orecchiette to the water and cook according to the instructions on the packet. Drain and set aside.
⊙ Heat the oil in a frying pan, then add the garlic and cook for 30 seconds. Add the lentils and cook for 2–3 minutes, or until they have warmed through. Stir the mint, balsamic vinegar, onion and basil through the lentils.
⊙ Toss the lentil mixture and green beans through the orecchiette, season with salt and pepper and sprinkle with the Feta. Serve.

Conchiglie with chicken and sage

This dish looks a little like a chicken bolognaise mixed through conchiglie, which is the shell-shaped pasta. I like to shave Parmesan in a big stack on the top and sprinkle it with dried shallots for bite. Serves 4.

250 g conchiglie

1 tablespoon olive oil

1 onion, chopped

3 chicken thigh fillets (500 g), finely
  chopped

1 1/2 tablespoons cider vinegar

2 tomatoes, peeled and chopped

1 teaspoon fresh sage, chopped

3/4 cup chicken stock

1/2 cup light cream

1 tablespoon chopped parsley

2 tablespoons grated Parmesan
  (optional)

1 tablespoon dried Asian shallots

⊙ Bring a large saucepan of salted water to the boil. Add the pasta and cook according to the instructions on the packet. Drain and set aside.
⊙ Heat the oil in a frying pan. Add the onion and cook until soft. Add the chicken and cook on high heat for about 5 minutes until browned. Add the vinegar, tomatoes, sage and stock. Simmer for 5 minutes.
⊙ Add the cream to the pan and simmer for about 3 minutes until it has thickened. Stir in the parsley and toss the mixture through the drained, cooked pasta. Sprinkle with the Parmesan and dried shallots and season with salt and pepper. Serve.

orecchiette with minted
lentils and Feta

Rigatoni with pumpkin, rocket and pine nuts

Simple, sassy and delicious hot or cold. A light, healthy, but filling meal. Serves 2–4.

500 g butternut pumpkin, peeled,
   deseeded and cut into 2 cm pieces
1/4 cup olive oil
150 g rigatoni
1/4 teaspoon chilli flakes
2 cloves garlic, chopped
1/3 cup rocket and Parmesan sauce
   (see below)
2 tablespoons toasted pine nuts
1 cup baby rocket leaves (60 g)
1 chilli, deseeded and sliced (optional)
Parmesan

⊙ Preheat the oven to 200°C.
⊙ In a bowl, toss the pumpkin cubes with
2 tablespoons of the olive oil. Season with salt and
pepper to taste and cook on a baking tray in the oven
for 30–40 minutes or until tender and browned. Set
aside.
⊙ Bring a large saucepan of salted water to the boil
and add the rigatoni. Cook according to the
instructions on the packet. Drain and set aside.
⊙ Heat the remaining oil in a frying pan. Add the chilli
flakes and garlic and cook for 30 seconds. Add the
rocket and Parmesan sauce, drained pasta and
pumpkin to the pan and cook until the pasta and
pumpkin have heated through. Remove from the heat
and toss with the pine nuts and rocket. Top with the
chilli and Parmesan shavings and serve.

Penne with oven-roasted ratatouille

Simple and delicious. Serves 2.

1 quantity ratatouille (see page 55)
160 g penne
1/3 cup pitted olives
Parmesan, shaved

⊙ Cook the penne according to the instructions on the
packet.
⊙ Warm the ratatouille (see page 55) in a wok or
saucepan over moderate heat and stir in the olives.
Toss the penne through and top with Parmesan
shavings. Serve.

Rocket and Parmesan sauce

*Sensational with finer pastas such as spaghettini, small shells or orecchiette, and with cold dishes like
pasta salad. Makes 1 cup of sauce.*

2 bunches fresh rocket
2 cloves garlic, roughly chopped
2 tablespoons pine nuts, lightly
   toasted
1/2 cup extra virgin olive oil
2 tablespoons grated Parmesan

⊙ Bring a large pot of salted water to the boil. Plunge
the rocket in and bring back to the boil. Drain and
refresh the rocket under cold water.
⊙ Place the rocket, garlic, pine nuts and olive oil in a
blender. Puree.
⊙ Scrape into a bowl and stir the Parmesan through,
along with a pinch of salt.

rigatoni with pumpkin,
rocket and pine nuts

macaroni cheese with
anchovies and rosemary

Macaroni cheese with anchovies and rosemary

After a surf or a run, I crave a solid meal and usually go for comfort food. Macaroni cheese is a sure-fire winner in that department. Another bonus is that it lasts about a week in the fridge for lazy food emergencies! Serves 4.

200 g ruote pazze (wagon-wheel pasta)
200 g low-fat ricotta
1/4 cup breadcrumbs
2 tablespoons grated Parmesan

For the béchamel sauce:
2 tablespoons low-fat margarine
2 tablespoons flour
3 cups low-fat milk
2 tomatoes, diced
3 anchovy fillets, finely chopped
1 teaspoon rosemary, chopped

⊙ Preheat the oven to 180°C.
⊙ Bring a large saucepan of salted water to the boil and cook the ruote pazze for about 2 minutes less than directed by the instructions on the packet. Drain and set aside.
⊙ For the béchamel sauce, melt the margarine in a medium-sized saucepan over moderate heat. Add the flour and stir for about 1 minute. Remove from the heat and slowly add the milk, stirring constantly with a whisk. When all the milk has been added, return the pan to the heat and slowly bring to a simmer, stirring with a wooden spoon, for 3–5 minutes. When thick, stir in the tomatoes, anchovies and rosemary. Season well with salt and pepper.
⊙ Lightly grease a baking dish. Pour half the béchamel sauce into the dish, cover with the pasta and the ricotta and add the remaining béchamel. Mix the breadcrumbs and Parmesan together and scatter over the top. Bake for 40 minutes, or until the top is golden.

Gianni's 'spag bol'

Italians traditionally use pork and veal mince for this dish, but beef works just as well. The carrot, celery and onion can be puréed in a food processor or blender rather than chopped, if desired. Eat with great friends, great wine and crusty Italian bread! Serves 6.

300 g spaghetti

For the sauce:
3 tablespoons olive oil
1 carrot, finely chopped
2 sticks celery, finely chopped
1 onion, finely chopped
1 kg beef mince (or half veal and half pork mince)
24 tablespoons tomato paste
1 cup red wine
2 x 420 g tinned crushed tomatoes

⊙ Heat the oil in a thick-based saucepan. Add the carrot, celery and onion, and cook over low heat for 10 minutes.
⊙ Increase the heat to high and add the mince. Cook, breaking up any lumps with a wooden spoon, until browned. Add the tomato paste and cook for 2 minutes, then add the wine and cook for a further 3 minutes.
⊙ Add the tomatoes, season well with salt and pepper, and simmer, covered and without stirring, for an hour or until a rich, red oil comes to the surface.
⊙ Cook the spaghetti according to the instructions on the packet and serve with the sauce.

In my opinion, tomatoes are the planet's most versatile fruit/vegetable. Whether raw, cooked, juiced, sauced, souped, fried, baked or barbecued; whether you choose Roma, egg, cherry, vine-ripened or sun-dried tomatoes, they add a smooth texture, rich taste and vibrant colour to any dish. Simply choose your tomato and get cooking!

tomatoes

Tomato, bread and chickpea soup

Amazing, amazing flavour! For a low-fat option, use plain toasted bread, but I think the oil-fried ciabatta is worth every calorie! Ciabatta is a crispy, traditional Italian oven-baked bread that can be found in most good bakeries or gourmet delis. Its waxy texture means it doesn't go soggy, which adds a wonderful chewy quality to this dish. Serves 3.

1/4 cup extra virgin olive oil

1 onion, sliced

3 cloves garlic, sliced

430 g tinned Roma tomatoes

5 fresh Roma tomatoes, peeled and sliced into quarters

300 g tinned chickpeas, drained and rinsed

2 cups chicken stock

3 thick slices of ciabatta bread fried in light olive oil

NOTE: If using dry chickpeas, soak 1 cup of chickpeas overnight in water, and drain before use.

○ Heat the olive oil in a large saucepan. Add the onion and garlic and cook over low heat until they are soft.

○ Add the tinned and fresh tomatoes, chickpeas and stock. Season with salt and pepper and simmer, uncovered, for 20 minutes.

○ Break the fried ciabatta and place in the bottom of 3 serving bowls. Top with the soup and drizzle with extra olive oil if desired. Serve.

Roasted tomato sauce

Mates will invite you to barbecues just so you'll bring this sauce! You can eat it with practically anything (or if you are my mate Zak – everything): chips, burgers, steak, eggs, polenta and pastas. You can also freeze it for up to two months. Makes 2 cups of sauce.

400 g tinned crushed tomatoes

4 large fresh tomatoes, quartered

1 onion, roughly chopped

6 cloves garlic, unpeeled

1/2 teaspoon fried chilli flakes

2 tablespoons olive oil

1 tablespoon brown sugar

1 tablespoon balsamic vinegar

NOTE: Lightly fry the dried chilli flakes in olive oil to release their flavour.

○ Preheat the oven to 220°C.

○ Place the tinned and fresh tomatoes, onion, garlic and chilli in a baking dish. Drizzle with the oil, season with salt and pepper and bake for 40 minutes, stirring occasionally. Sprinkle with the brown sugar and balsamic vinegar and bake for a further 10 minutes.

○ Cool for a few minutes, then remove the garlic from its skin and purée everything in a food processor. Serve.

tomato, bread and chickpea soup

stuffed roasted tomatoes

Stuffed roasted tomatoes

These make a great entrée or side dish with a salad. Makes 2 stuffed tomatoes.

2 whole tomatoes
1 clove garlic, chopped
2 teaspoons mixed herbs, chopped
   (basil, thyme and parsley work
   well)
4 teaspoons breadcrumbs
2 teaspoons Parmesan (or your
   favourite hard cheese), grated
olive oil

⊙ Preheat the oven to 170°C.
⊙ Slice the tops off the tomatoes and set them aside. Remove the core and seeds and discard. Sprinkle the garlic and mixed herbs over both tomatoes, followed by the breadcrumbs and grated Parmesan. Drizzle with olive oil and season with salt and pepper.
⊙ Replace the tops of the tomatoes and roast for about an hour or until very soft. Serve.

Ratatouille

This dish gets a lot of action! I serve it over the top of grilled fish or as a bed under a lean cut of grilled lamb. It goes beautifully with penne or conchiglie and is also spectacular on its own. Makes 2 cups.

¼ cup olive oil
1 tablespoon tomato paste
1 large eggplant, cut into 2 cm cubes
2 zucchini, sliced into thick rounds
2 brown onion, cut into thick wedges
2 red capsicum, deseeded, cut into
   thick strips and chopped
2 cloves garlic, chopped
2 teaspoons mixed Italian herbs or
1 tablespoon fresh thyme and a bay
   leaf
5 Roma tomatoes, quartered
425 g tinned diced tomatoes
1 tablespoon capers
1 teaspoon orange zest
2 tablespoons chopped parsley

⊙ Preheat the oven to 200°C.
⊙ In a large bowl, combine the oil, tomato paste, eggplant, zucchini, onion, capsicum, garlic, herbs and fresh tomatoes. Toss and pour these into a large baking dish. Roast for 45 minutes, making sure the vegetables at the edge of the pan don't burn. Add the tinned tomatoes, stir well and roast for a further 15 minutes.
⊙ Stir the capers, orange zest and parsley through the ratatouille and roast for a further 5 minutes. Season well with salt and pepper. Serve.

Oven-dried tomato and Parmesan salad

When you roast tomatoes, you trap the seasonings like salt, pepper, garlic and lemon in the flesh. Depending on the season, tomatoes can be lacking in flavour, so this serves to permeate them with spices, with mouth-watering results. Serves 4.

4 vine-ripened tomatoes
2 cloves garlic, sliced
1 teaspoon thyme leaves
1/2 teaspoon sugar
2 tablespoons extra virgin olive oil
1 tablespoon lemon juice
2 cups baby spinach or rocket
1/4 cup Parmesan shavings

- Preheat the oven to 170°C.
- Quarter the tomatoes and remove the core. Sprinkle the garlic, thyme and sugar over the tomato quarters and season well with salt and pepper. Place the tomatoes on a baking tray lined with baking paper.
- Roast for 45 minutes or until the flesh is slightly yellowed and dried, and a little shrivelled at the edges.
- In a bowl, combine the oil and lemon juice. Toss the spinach or rocket with the lemon and oil and place on a plate. Top with the tomatoes and sprinkle with Parmesan. Serve.

Tomato and basil salad

This simple salad is also beautiful with fresh, sliced bocconcini, kalamata olives and sprinkled with Parmesan shavings. Serves 2.

4 vine-ripened tomatoes, sliced
1/3 cup loosely packed basil leaves
1 clove garlic, crushed
1 tablespoon balsamic vinegar
3 tablespoons olive oil

- Arrange the tomatoes and basil on a plate.
- In a bowl, combine the garlic, balsamic vinegar and olive oil. Drizzle over the tomatoes and serve.

Jase's 2 cents
Roasted whole tomatoes

To skin tomatoes before roasting, cut a cross in the base of the tomato. Place it in a bowl and pour boiling water over it. Drain and refresh under cold water, then peel it and place on an oven tray. Roast at 200°C for 30 minutes, or until slightly blistered.

oven-dried tomato
and Parmesan salad

Chicken is high in protein, low in fat and rich in flavour. I like to cook with corn-fed and free-range chickens.

FREE RANGE A truly free-range chicken is raised in uncrowded conditions with clean water free of chlorine or fluorides, fresh air, and access to sunlight. They are not fed antibiotics, coccidiostats or artificial growth stimulants.

CORN FED/ORGANIC These chickens are fed on wholesome grains, corn and legumes – 100 per cent organic grains grown without pesticides, fungicides, herbicides or synthetic plant regulators. They are raised without antibiotics or synthetic growth hormones. No chlorine is used in the chilling process.

Here are some simple ways you can make chicken dishes even better for you:
- Trim all visible fat before preparation.
- Enhance the natural flavour with herbs and spices.
- Try using flavoured vinegars, wines, soy sauce and citrus juices.
- Try using low-sodium ingredients and salt substitutes to eliminate sodium without sacrificing flavour in the recipes.
- Use chicken as a substitute for red meat in favourite recipes to lower fat and calorie content. For example, use chicken patties instead of regular ground beef or pork in burgers.
- Boil, roast, bake, grill or poach chicken, or sauté it in a small amount of chicken broth.
- Use non-stick cooking sprays or olive oil for pan frying.

chicken

Chicken breast stuffed with greens

For this recipe you need chicken breasts with the skin still intact. I like to serve this one over a bed of steamed asparagus or steamed chat potatoes. Serves 2.

1 cup continental flat-leaf parsley
  leaves
2 cups baby English spinach leaves
1 cup baby rocket leaves
2 cloves garlic, chopped
2 chicken breasts (160 g each), skin
  still on
1 tablespoon butter, melted
1 tablespoon olive oil

○ Preheat the oven to 200°C.

○ Rinse the parsley, spinach and rocket and place in a medium-sized frying pan. Cook over moderate heat, covered and shaking the pan occasionally, for 2–3 minutes or until the ingredients have wilted. (If you want you can do this in a bowl covered with plastic wrap in the microwave. After cooking, squeeze out any excess water and chop roughly.)

○ Using your fingers, gently separate the chicken skin from the flesh. Stuff the wilted greens under the skin.

○ Heat the butter and oil in an ovenproof frying pan over high heat. Cook the chicken breast side down for 3 minutes. Turn the chicken breasts over and place the pan in the oven. Cook for a further 5 minutes, or until cooked through. Season with salt and pepper and serve.

Stir-fried chicken with ginger and snow peas

Serves 4.

3 chicken thigh fillets (about 500 g),
  skin removed, thinly sliced
2 tablespoons soy sauce
1 teaspoon sesame oil
1 tablespoon shaoxing wine
2 teaspoons cornflour
1 tablespoon peanut oil
1 tablespoon ginger, cut into
  matchstick-thin strips
2 cloves garlic, finely chopped
1 cup pumpkin (or leftover roasted
  pumpkin), thinly sliced
1 cup snow peas, trimmed and halved
3 tablespoons oyster sauce
¼ cup chicken stock
2 shallots, sliced on the diagonal into
  2 cm pieces
1 quantity cooked rice (see page 6)

○ In a bowl, combine the chicken with 1 tablespoon of the soy sauce, the sesame oil, shaoxing wine and cornflour. Mix well and set aside to marinate for about 10 minutes.

○ Heat the peanut oil in a wok. Add the ginger and garlic and stir-fry for about a minute. Then add the pumpkin and chicken (discard the marinade) and stir-fry for about 5 minutes until the chicken is browned.

○ Add the snow peas, the remaining soy sauce, oyster sauce and stock. Stir-fry for an extra minute, then stir in the shallots. Serve with cooked rice.

NOTE: If you don't have shaoxing wine, you can use dry sherry.

chicken breast stuffed with greens

chicken poached with tarragon, used here
in chicken, green bean and potato salad

Chicken poached with tarragon

This dish melts in the mouth, and the best part is the whole thing takes less than 20 minutes to prepare. In the photograph, this dish is used in chicken, green bean and potato salad (see page 36). Serves 3.

3 small chicken breasts (500 g)
3 cups water
1¼ cups verjuice
1 teaspoon salt
1 teaspoon dry tarragon

NOTE: If you don't have verjuice, you can also use 1¼ cups dry white wine.

○ Place the chicken breasts in a medium-sized saucepan with the water, verjuice, salt and tarragon and bring to the boil.
○ As soon as the mixture boils, remove from the heat, cover and let cool in the liquid, ideally for about half an hour.
○ Slice and serve the chicken on sandwiches, or in chicken, green bean and potato salad (see page 36).

Chicken with Jerusalem artichokes

A one-pot wonder! This dish is like a chicken stew with a tantalising grilled cheese gratin as a lid. Serves 2.

4 chicken legs, skin removed
1 tablespoon flour, seasoned with
  salt and pepper
1 tablespoon olive oil
1 onion, chopped
6 small Jerusalem artichokes,
  scrubbed
2 cups chicken stock
½ teaspoon ground fennel seeds
½ cup baby spinach leaves
6 spears asparagus (150 g), halved
2 tablespoons breadcrumbs
2 tablespoons grated Swiss cheese
  or Parmesan
1 tablespoon chopped parsley

○ Dust the chicken lightly with the flour. Heat the oil in a medium-sized frying pan. Cook the chicken through and set it aside.
○ Add the onion to the pan and cook until soft and browned. Then return the chicken to the pan and add the Jerusalem artichokes, chicken stock and fennel seeds. Bring to the boil, reduce the heat and cook, covered, for about 40 minutes, or until the chicken and artichokes are tender. Stir in the spinach leaves and asparagus and cook for a further 2 minutes.
○ Preheat the griller. Transfer the chicken to two shallow, ovenproof serving bowls. Sprinkle with the breadcrumbs and cheese and grill until brown. Top with the parsley and serve immediately.

Tuscan-style spatchcock

A great light meal, and you can substitute the spatchcock with chicken if you like. A tip for cooking spatchcock or chicken, if you're feeding more than two people it is a good idea to use a whole chook (1.2–3 kg). Cooking time will vary with size. I like to serve this dish with wedges of iceberg lettuce drizzled with lemon juice and olive oil. Serves 1.

1 spatchcock
2 sage leaves
2 tablespoons olive oil
2 cloves garlic, peeled and bruised

○ Cut the spatchcock from neck to tail down the backbone and flatten by fanning each side out like wings.

○ Carefully push the sage leaves under the skin. Season well with salt and pepper and drizzle with some of the olive oil.

○ Heat the remaining olive oil in a thick-based frying pan. Add the garlic and place the spatchcock skin side down. Cover with a heavy lid slightly smaller than the pan – this will keep the spatchcock flat while cooking. Cook over medium heat for 5 minutes, then turn the spatchcock and replace the lid. Cook for a further 4 minutes or until the skin is crisp and the meat cooked through. Serve.

Chicken and celeriac fricassee

Celeriac is a root vegetable with a distinct celery flavour. It is now available in some supermarkets and fruit and veg shops. If you can find it, try it. If not, substitute it with another root vegetable such as parsnip or even potato. Serve with brightly coloured mixed steamed vegies. Serves 4.

1 tablespoon olive oil
4 chicken thigh fillets (500 g),
   quartered
2 rashers bacon
6 small pearl onions, halved
1 large head celeriac (500 g), peeled
   and cut into small wedges
2 tablespoons flour
2 cups chicken stock
1/4 cup low-fat cream
2 teaspoons marjoram,
   chopped (optional)
1 tablespoon chopped parsley

○ Heat the oil in a deep-sided frying pan. Brown the chicken on both sides but do not cook through. Remove it and set aside.

○ Add the bacon, onions and celeriac to the pan and cook until browned. Sprinkle the flour over the pan and cook, stirring, for 1 minute. Then slowly add the stock, stirring until the mixture thickens slightly. Return the chicken to the pan. Season with salt and pepper and cook over medium heat, covered, for 15 minutes.

○ Add the cream and marjoram if using. Simmer, uncovered, for another 5 minutes until the liquid has thickened. Stir the parsley through and serve.

chicken and celeriac fricassee

chicken and celery broth

Chicken with tarragon and vinegar

This one is very fragrant, so serve it immediately after cooking. It also keeps well in the fridge and it will freeze for a few weeks too, provided you take out the asparagus spears before storing, as they tend to go mushy. Add fresh spears when you reheat it. Serves 4.

4 chicken thigh fillets, boned and
   skinned, fat and sinew removed
1 teaspoon flour
1 tablespoon olive oil
3 sprigs fresh tarragon
1½ tablespoons white wine vinegar
½ cup salt-reduced chicken stock
1 orange, juice and zest
12 spears asparagus
1 tablespoon light cream
freshly ground pepper

Split the chicken thighs in half widthways and place in a bag with the flour. Coat the chicken pieces evenly.

Heat the oil in a sauté pan or small, high-sided frying pan. Cook the chicken lightly until evenly coloured and cooked through.

Add half the leaves from the tarragon stalks and the vinegar. Stir in the stock and the orange zest and bring to a simmer. Cover with a tight-fitting lid and cook gently for 15–20 minutes, stirring occasionally.

Blanch the asparagus in boiling water for about 3 minutes or until tender, then remove it and refresh under cold running water till cool. Slice the stalks into thirds.

Remove the chicken from the pan and set it aside, keeping it warm. Turn the heat up and cook until the sauce has reduced by half. Stir in the orange juice and allow to simmer for 1 minute, then bring back to the boil.

Stir in the cream and add the chicken, asparagus and remaining tarragon leaves. Season with cracked pepper and serve.

Chicken and celery broth

Chicken soup is everyone's favourite pick-me-up. With chickpeas and big, solid chicken pieces, this is a really satisfying meal – especially in winter. I like to serve it in a huge mug. Serves 2.

1 tablespoon olive oil
1 onion, chopped
1 clove garlic, sliced
2 stalks celery, sliced
3 cups chicken stock
2 chicken legs, skin removed
300 g tinned chickpeas, drained and
   rinsed
1 tablespoon chopped parsley

Heat the oil in a medium-sized saucepan and add the onion, garlic and celery. Cook over medium heat until soft, then add the stock and chicken legs. Bring to the boil, reduce the heat and simmer, covered, for about 40 minutes or until the chicken is tender.

Take the pan off the heat. Remove chicken from the pan and set it aside to cool for a few minutes. When cool enough, remove the flesh from the bone.

Return the chicken flesh to the broth and add the chickpeas. Simmer for about 5 minutes or until the chicken and chickpeas have warmed through. Season well with salt and pepper and garnish with the parsley. Serve.

I am a huge advocate of eating red meat. I love it. A great steak, snag or cut of lamb cooked to perfection is mouth-watering and always hits the spot!

And, eaten in moderation, red meat is good for you. It contains iron for energy and better concentration, protein for growth, development and repair, zinc to promote a healthy immune system, vitamin B12 to maintain your nervous system and omega 3 to sustain a healthy heart.

So get into your lean lamb and beef and enjoy these nutritious and tasty recipes.

beef & lamb

Grilled sirloin steak with tarragon butter

I think this is one of the 'freshest' ways to serve steak; a tapenade or salsa-style finish gives it real summer appeal. Serves 1 and makes about 10 serves of butter.

For the steak:
200 g sirloin steak, cut into 4 pieces
1 tablespoon olive tapenade
1 tomato, seeded and diced

For the tarragon butter:
250 g softened unsalted butter (not
  melted)
1 small bunch tarragon leaves (15 g),
  chopped
juice of half a lemon

To make the tarragon butter:
◎ Prepare the butter in advance, as it requires refrigeration before serving. Beat the butter by hand or in a food processor till it's soft and creamy. Add the tarragon, lemon juice, salt and pepper and stir to combine.
◎ Spread the butter mixture evenly onto a piece of foil and roll it up to form a log about 3 cm across. Twist the ends. Refrigerate the butter until firm. Cut into 0.5 cm rounds when ready to use. The butter will last up to 3 months in the freezer provided it is well wrapped.

To cook the steak:
◎ Season the steak pieces with salt and pepper, then cook on a griddle for 4–6 minutes on each side or until cooked to your liking. Remove and allow the pieces to sit for 3–4 minutes.
◎ Preheat the grill. Spread the steak pieces with olive tapenade, and top with the diced tomato. Slice 4 rounds of the tarragon butter, and top each piece of steak with a round. Place the steaks under the grill until the butter has almost melted. Serve immediately.

Fillet steak with eschalot and red wine sauce

A hearty one, great with a Margaret River Cab Sav. Serves 2.

2 x 150 g fillet steaks
1 tablespoon olive oil
30 g butter
2 eschalots, finely chopped
2 teaspoons red wine vinegar (or any
  vinegar if you don't have this one)
1/4 cup red wine
1/2 cup beef or chicken stock
1 tablespoon parsley, finely chopped

◎ Season the steaks with salt and pepper. Heat the oil and 1 teaspoon of the butter in a medium-sized frying pan. Cook the steaks for 3–5 minutes on each side or until cooked to your liking. Remove and keep warm (a good way is to put them on a plate and cover with foil).
◎ To make the sauce, add the eschalots to the pan and cook until soft. Pour in the vinegar and red wine and cook for a further 30 seconds. Then add the stock and simmer for 2 minutes. Whisk in the rest of the butter and the parsley for 20–30 seconds until mixed through. Serve the sauce over the steak.

grilled sirloin steak with tarragon butter

corned beef with white sauce

Corned beef with white sauce

Your classic meat and three veg! Leftover corned beef can be used in bubble and squeak (see page 33) or in toasted sandwiches (see page 125). Serves 4–6.

For the beef:

1 kg piece corned beef

1 onion, roughly chopped

1 carrot, roughly chopped

2 tablespoons white wine vinegar

1½ tablespoons brown sugar

2 bay leaves

½ teaspoon peppercorns

For the white sauce:

2 tablespoons butter

1 small onion, finely chopped

1½ tablespoons plain flour

2 cups milk

a pinch ground cloves

a pinch nutmeg

pepper

¼ cup cooking broth from the
   corned silverside

○ Place the corned beef, onion and carrot in a large saucepan. Cover with water and add the vinegar, brown sugar, bay leaves and peppercorns. Bring to the boil, then reduce the heat to low and simmer gently, covered, for 2 hours or until the meat is tender.

○ To make the white sauce, melt the butter over medium heat, then add the onion and cook until soft. Sprinkle the flour over the onion and cook, stirring, for 1 minute. Remove the pan from the heat and slowly whisk in milk. Return to the heat and gradually bring to the boil, stirring until thick. Season with the cloves, nutmeg and pepper, and stir in the cooking broth.

○ Slice the corned beef into chunks and serve with the carrots, as well as beans, potatoes and the white sauce.

Jose's 2 cents Meat

• If you are using cheap cuts (eg, chuck steak or blade steak) you need to allow extra cooking time for the best flavour and texture possible.

• Expensive cuts save you time overall, as they are already lush, lean and tender. You can sear them in seconds.

Fillet steak with mushroom sauce

An old favourite. Serve with anything from 'Bit on the side' (see page 104) or with a huge stack of steamed green string beans. Serves 2.

1 tablespoon olive oil

2 x 160 g fillet steaks

2 teaspoons butter

2 cloves garlic, crushed

160 g mixed mushrooms (a
   combination of button, shiitake and
   chestnut is lovely), quartered

1 teaspoon dried thyme

½ cup sour cream

○ Heat the oil in a medium-sized frying pan, then add the steaks and cook on high heat for 3–5 minutes on each side or until cooked to your liking. Remove and keep them warm under foil. Reduce the heat to moderate.

○ To make the sauce, add the butter and garlic to the pan and cook for 1 minute. Add the mushrooms and cook until soft, then add the thyme and sour cream and cook for 2 minutes, or until the cream has thickened slightly. Season with salt and pepper and serve over the steaks.

Mum's rissoles

These rissoles are one of my earliest childhood memories. Mum used to make masses of them and we'd eat about a third that day and the rest would last all week. We'd have them reheated with vegies, fried with tomato sauce, on burgers, as snacks and for school lunches. They're absolutely delicious served with stuffed roasted tomatoes (see page 55). Makes 12 rissoles.

500 g lean beef mince, well chilled

1 onion, finely chopped

3 slices of bread with crusts, cut into 1 cm cubes

1 egg

2 tablespoons Worcestershire sauce

1 teaspoon ground black pepper

1 teaspoon salt

1 teaspoon mixed herbs (rosemary and parsley is nice)

½ cup flour

½ cup water

extra flour to coat the rissoles

1 tablespoon cooking oil

○ Using your hands, mix the mince, onion, bread cubes, egg, Worcestershire sauce, spices, flour and water in a large bowl till well mixed and emulsified.

○ With wet hands, take small handfuls of the mince and roll into golf-ball-sized rounds. Then roll each through the flour to give it a thin coating and dust off any excess flour.

○ Heat the oil in a thick-based pan with a tight-fitting lid. When the oil is hot, place the rissoles in the pan and cook, turning them, until golden. Then cover and allow them to cook for a further 5–6 minutes or until they are firm to touch. Serve.

Bangers and beans

Sausages with personality! Any snags will do. This dish keeps for a day or two in the fridge and reheats in minutes. Serves 4.

1 tablespoon olive oil

4 good quality Italian sausages

1 onion, sliced

2 cloves garlic, sliced

1 carrot, chopped

½ cup red wine

430 g tinned tomatoes

400 g tinned beans (borlotti or cannellini)

3 tablespoons chopped parsley

○ Heat the oil in a frying pan. Add the sausages and cook until browned. Remove and set aside.

○ If the sausages are fatty, drain the excess oil from the pan, then add the onion, garlic and carrot. Cook until all have browned. Add the wine and cook for 1 minute, then add the tomatoes and beans and cook for a further minute.

○ Return the sausages to the pan, season with salt and pepper and simmer for 20 minutes. Stir the parsley through and serve.

Mum's rissoles

minute steak niçoise style

Minute steak niçoise style

Too easy! This would have to be one of the simplest, tastiest meals I could offer to all those meat eaters out there, and if you're vegetarian, you can substitute the meat with an assortment of grilled vegetables, for example mushrooms, zucchini, capsicum and artichokes. Niçoise is the name given to various dishes typical to the region of Nice in France. These dishes are known for their use of garlic, olives, anchovies, tomatoes and French green beans. Serves 2.

300 g beef fillet

1 tablespoon olive oil

1 tablespoon butter

3 cloves garlic, finely sliced

3 anchovy fillets, finely chopped

2 tomatoes, blanched, refreshed, peeled and finely chopped

1/4 cup small black olives

2 tablespoons chopped flat-leaf parsley

200 g green beans, blanched till tender then refreshed under cold water

- Thinly slice the meat into pieces about 5 mm thick, remembering to cut against the grain rather than with the grain. Season with salt and pepper.
- Heat the oil and butter in a large, thick-based saucepan. Add the garlic and anchovies and cook until the garlic starts to colour.
- Add the meat and proceed to brown it, making sure the garlic doesn't burn. Turn after about 30 seconds and repeat. After about 20 seconds on the second side, throw in the chopped tomato, olives and parsley.
- Remove the meat and set it aside. Throw in the beans, giving the pan a good toss to mix them with the sauce. Cook for about 30 seconds. Serve the meat on top of the sauce. If you want to bulk out this dish, throw in a handful of chopped, steamed potatoes with the beans.

Braised beef with turnips and mint

Some meals are worth spending a little extra time on, and this is one of them. Serves 4–6.

1 teaspoon butter

1 teaspoon olive oil

1 kg beef shank, bone removed

200 g fatty bacon, cut into batons

3 brown onions, finely sliced

2 carrots, peeled and cut into bite-size chunks

2 large turnips, peeled and cut into bite-size chunks

1 cup red wine

2/3 cup cider vinegar

1 cup water

a bunch aromatic herbs including thyme, mint, bay leaves and parsley, tied into a tight bouquet with a piece of string

- Heat the butter and oil in a large, thick-based saucepan with a tight-fitting lid. Season the shank meat well with salt and pepper, and brown on all sides in the pan. Remove and set aside.
- Add the bacon to the pan and cook until browned, then add the onion and continue to cook till it's soft and translucent.
- Add the remaining vegetables along with the wine, vinegar, water, herbs and the browned meat. Bring to the boil and then reduce the heat to a very low simmer. Cook for 2–2 1/2 hours. The meat is ready when you can push a skewer or sharp knife into it with no resistance.
- Adjust the seasoning to taste, remove the herb bouquet and tear up the mint and parsley before returning it to the pan. Serve with mashed potato and a bread stick.

Lamb cutlets with anchovy and rosemary sauce

Chops with a twist! I stack spoonfuls of crushed potatoes on a bed of bright green steamed spinach, then throw the chops over the top and sprinkle with sea salt. Serves 1.

2 tablespoons olive oil

3 x 60 g lamb cutlets

3 anchovy fillets, finely chopped

1 clove garlic, crushed

juice of half a lemon

1/2 tablespoon rosemary, finely chopped

○ Heat 1 tablespoon of the oil in a medium-sized frying pan. Add the cutlets and cook for 2–3 minutes on each side or until cooked to your liking. Remove and set aside.

○ To make the sauce, add the anchovies and garlic to the pan and fry for 1 minute. Then add the lemon juice and rosemary, and slowly add the remaining olive oil over about a minute. Serve the sauce over the cutlets.

Lamb shanks in pinot noir

This winning winter classic is fit for a Viking. I like to serve the meat in a shallow bowl with the remaining juices over the top. Serves 2.

2 tablespoons olive oil

4 x 180 g lamb shanks

1 onion, roughly chopped

1 small stick celery, roughly chopped

1 carrot, roughly chopped

3 cloves garlic, crushed

1/4 cup tomato paste

2 cups red wine (pinot noir is best)

4 cups beef or chicken stock

1 tablespoon rosemary, chopped

6 chat potatoes, halved if large

2 x 5 cm strips orange zest, white pith removed

1/2 cup pitted black olives

2 tablespoons chopped parsley

NOTE: Thinly peel the orange zest with a knife instead of a grater or zester to get the length required.

○ Heat the oil in a large, thick-based saucepan. Cook the lamb in batches until browned. Remove and set aside.

○ Add the onion, celery, carrot and garlic to the pan and cook over low heat until soft. Add the tomato paste and cook, stirring, for 1 minute. Pour in the wine and stock and add the rosemary. Bring to the boil and return the lamb shanks to the pan. (You may need more or less stock, depending on the size of your saucepan. Just make sure the liquid covers the shanks while cooking.) Add the potato, zest and olives. Reduce the heat to a very low simmer and cook, covered, for 2 hours.

○ Stir the parsley through and serve with creamed silver beet (see page 117).

lamb cutlets with anchovy
and rosemary sauce

lamb's fry with pickled beetroot

Lamb with butter beans and eggplant

The 20-minute meal. A Mediterranean meat-pot that serves 4.

180–220 g lamb loin, trimmed of fat and sinew

3 tablespoons olive oil

1 small eggplant, cut into 1 cm cubes

400 g tinned butter beans, well drained

2 tomatoes, roughly chopped

1/2 cup chicken stock or water

1 small chilli, finely chopped

a few leaves fresh mint, torn

◉ Cut the lamb loin into small, bite-size pieces and season with salt and pepper. Heat a tablespoon of the oil in a frying pan over high heat. When the oil begins to smoke, add the lamb pieces and sauté till they're golden. Remove and set them aside.

◉ Lower the heat and add the remaining oil and the eggplant. Cook over a gentle heat for 8–10 minutes, turning frequently. The eggplant should soften but not turn to mush.

◉ Add the butter beans, tomatoes, stock and chilli. Use a fork to crush some of the beans to help thicken the sauce.

◉ After 5 minutes of gentle simmering, add the lamb and mint and cover with a lid or foil. Turn the heat off and allow the lamb to steep for 5 minutes before serving. It may need a little more seasoning.

Lamb's fry with pickled beetroot

Some of us would kill for a good lamb's fry meal, but for those of you who are not that way inclined, go for the pickled beetroot. It's brilliant as a little salad served on a bed of rocket. Serves 2.

For the beetroot:

3 tablespoons olive oil

3 medium beetroot, peeled and finely sliced or grated

1 tablespoon brown sugar

3 tablespoons balsamic vinegar

1/4 teaspoon ground cloves

1/4 cup water

For the meat:

1 tablespoon olive oil

a knob butter

350 g lamb's liver, cut into 0.5 cm slices

2 tablespoons flour

For the beetroot:

◉ Heat the oil in a medium-sized saucepan, add the beetroot and cook for 2–3 minutes. Add the sugar, balsamic vinegar and cloves and season with salt and pepper. Cook for a further minute and then pour in the water. Cover and cook for 5 minutes. Strain and set aside.

For the meat:

◉ Heat the oil and butter in a thick-based frying pan. Lightly dust the liver pieces with the flour and season with salt and pepper. Cook for 1 minute on each side, or until cooked to your liking.

◉ Serve, using the beetroot as a bed for the lamb's fry. This is also very tasty served with fried firm polenta (see page 22).

Roasted lamb rump and garlic with walnuts

This is my 'very modern' roast, with cubed chats, walnuts and chewy, roasted garlic. Serves 2.

1/3 cup walnuts
2 chat potatoes, cubed
4 pearl onions, halved
6 cloves garlic, skin still on
2 tablespoons olive oil
2 x 180 g lamb rumps
2 teaspoons walnut oil
1/4 cup white wine

- Preheat the oven to 170°C.
- On an oven tray, roast the walnuts for 10 minutes or until golden. Remove and increase the oven heat to 200°C. Cool the walnuts for a few minutes before chopping roughly.
- In a bowl, toss together the potatoes, onions, garlic and 1 tablespoon of oil. Season well with salt and pepper. Tip the contents of the bowl into an ovenproof dish and roast for 25–30 minutes or until the potatoes are golden and cooked through.
- Rub the lamb with the walnut oil and season with salt and pepper. Heat the remaining tablespoon of oil in a frying pan and sear the lamb flesh side down until rare but not cooked through. Transfer the lamb to the dish with the potatoes for the last 12 minutes of roasting.
- When cooked, remove the meat and set it aside to rest. Toss the walnuts through the potatoes. Slice the lamb and serve with the potatoes.

Seafood no longer means just another prawn on the barbecue. Living on the world's biggest island, surrounded by clean, healthy oceans means we are privileged to have access to some of the freshest seafood on the globe. It tastes fabulous and it's healthy, too!

Seafood is packed with key long-chain omega 3 fatty acids, which help prevent coronary heart disease. It is generally low in cholesterol and high in vitamins, protein and minerals.

So go ahead, throw another king prawn on the barbie – next to the salmon, marinated octopus, crumbed calamari and sumptuous snapper!

fish & seafood

Seared scallops with celeriac and snow pea salad

I like to serve this beautiful salad piled high on a large, flat dish. Make the salad first, as it needs to sit for 30 minutes before serving. Serves 2.

1 heaped tablespoon whole egg
  mayonnaise
1 teaspoon Dijon mustard
1 small head celeriac (about 350 g)
1 tablespoon lemon or lime juice
50 g snow peas
160 g fresh scallops, not frozen
1 teaspoon olive oil
1 small handful fresh rocket or baby
  spinach

For the salad:
- In a small bowl, mix together the mayonnaise, mustard, salt and pepper to make a rémoulade.
- Remove the thick skin of the celeriac, as you would to peel the rind of an orange. Finely cut it into 2–3 mm slices, then cut the slices into thin matchsticks.
- Add the celeriac to the rémoulade and pour in the lemon juice. Mix well to combine.
- The snow peas can be shredded raw, or dipped into boiling water for 20 seconds then refreshed under cold water and shredded, which will allow them to keep their colour and texture. Add them to the celeriac, mix well and allow to sit for a good half hour before serving.

For the scallops:
- Season the scallops with salt and pepper.
- Heat a thick-based pan or griddle till very hot, then moisten with the oil and sear the scallops for 20–30 seconds on each side depending on their size. Don't overcrowd the pan or the scallops will stew.
- Toss the scallops lightly through the salad, add a small handful of rocket leaves and serve.

Snapper in a bag

This may sound strange, but it's foolproof and so bloody magical that you will get more mileage out of it than almost anything else you cook. It's a bachelor's paradise – it impresses on all fronts and makes you look like a pro! Serves 1.

180 g snapper fillet
1 cup cabbage braised with apples
  and white wine (see page 114)
olive oil

NOTE: If you don't make the cabbage recipe, the fish can also be cooked with mixed vegetables or English spinach.

- Preheat the oven to 200°C.
- Place the cabbage in an oven bag (these can be bought in the supermarket, but if you don't have one, wrap the ingredients securely in foil). Put the snapper on top of the cabbage. Drizzle with olive oil and tie the bag.
- Cook for 12–15 minutes. Open the bag and serve.

snapper in a bag

prawn, grapefruit
and avocado salad

Prawn, grapefruit and avocado salad

A sizzling summer lunch special. Serves 2.

2 rashers of bacon, rind removed,
  cut into batons
1 small ripe avocado
1 ruby red grapefruit
2 tablespoons olive oil
2 tablespoons white wine vinegar
10 medium-sized prawns, cooked,
  shelled and deveined
1 small head of radicchio or other
  bitter lettuce, washed and
  separated

*NOTE: If your prawns aren't already
cooked, throw them into a pot of
boiling, salted water and simmer
gently for 1–2 minutes. Remove and
allow to cool at room temperature.*

○ In a thick-based frying pan, fry the bacon until golden and crisp. Remove from the pan and drain on absorbent paper.
○ Split the avocado in half and remove the stone. Using a large spoon, remove the flesh from the skin, trying to keep the avocado intact. Slice into similarly sized pieces.
○ Segment the grapefruit, removing the pith. Once the segments have been set aside, squeeze what's left of the grapefruit into a small bowl to make the dressing.
○ Add the oil, white wine vinegar and salt and pepper to the grapefruit juice and stir to combine.
○ Assemble the prawns, avocado, grapefruit, bacon and radicchio in a salad bowl and drizzle the dressing over the top.

Red curry of barramundi

This basic red curry sauce can also be used with beef, chicken or vegetables. Serves 2.

1 cup coconut cream
1–1½ tablespoons good quality red
  curry paste
1½ cups coconut milk
1½ tablespoons fish sauce
1½ tablespoons palm sugar or
  brown sugar
1 star anise
2 x 150 g barramundi fillets, cut into
  large chunks
juice of 1 lime
4 lime leaves, thinly sliced
⅓ cup Thai or purple basil leaves

○ Place the coconut cream in a wok or large frying pan and cook, stirring, over high heat for about 5 minutes or until the oil separates from the cream. Add the curry paste and stir for another minute, or until fragrant. Slowly add the coconut milk, fish sauce, palm sugar and star anise. Simmer for about 15 minutes, or until red oil comes to the surface.
○ Add the barramundi fillets and lime juice. Cook gently for about 5 minutes. Stir the lime and basil leaves through and serve immediately over hot steamed white rice, with plenty of the liquid drizzled over the top.

Pan-roasted salmon with mustard potatoes

Roasting salmon with the skin on over a low, gentle heat, gives a crispy texture on the outside, a soft taste sensation on the inside and an aesthetically pleasing finish. Serves 2.

2 tablespoons olive oil
2 salmon fillets, each about 180 g,
　bones removed
mustard potatoes (see page 36)

○ Heat the oil in a frying pan over low heat. Season the salmon with salt and pepper and place the fillets skin side down in the pan. Cook for 2 minutes on each side for rare, depending on how thick the pieces are. Cook for longer if desired.
○ Serve with mustard potatoes (see page 36).

Tempura prawns with fennel and aioli

I like to keep fried food to a minimum, but you have to treat yourself now and then! Tempura is the perfect way, and you can tempura almost anything – sweets, seafood, meat and vegies. My friend Alison taught me her show-off method of using a simple egg carton to drain any excess oil from the tempura after frying (see picture). It's pretty ingenious – thanks Al! Serves 2.

For the tempura prawns:
1 cup tempura flour
1 egg yolk
1 cup iced water (it can even have
　cubes of ice in it)
oil for deep frying (mono-unsaturated
　is best – canola or sunflower oil)
12 medium-sized, raw prawns,
　peeled, deveined, tails still on
1 baby fennel, sliced thinly

NOTE: Tempura flour is a widely available flour mix, but cornflour can be used if you can't get hold of it.

For the aioli:
2/3 cup whole egg mayonnaise
juice of 1 lemon
2 cloves garlic, crushed

○ To make the tempura batter, place the flour, egg yolk and water in a bowl. Stir until they are lightly combined and still lumpy.
○ Pour oil into a wok or thick-based saucepan until it's about one-third full. Heat until a cube of bread browns in 15 seconds.
○ Quickly dip the prawns and fennel in the tempura batter. Cook in batches in the oil until crisp; about 1–2 minutes each.
○ To make the aioli, mix the mayonnaise, lemon juice and garlic together and serve with the tempura prawns.

tempura pawns
with fennel and aioli

Parmesan-crusted flathead

Mussels with chilli and crème fraiche

Serves 2.

30 g butter
1 onion, peeled and finely sliced
¾ cups dry, acidic white wine
  (preferably Muscadet)
700 g mussels, scrubbed and
  debearded
2 bird's eye chillies, seeds removed
  and finely chopped
2 ripe tomatoes, skinned, seeded
  and coarsely chopped
2 tablespoons crème fraiche or sour
  cream
¼ bunch chopped flat parsley
black pepper

⊙ Melt the butter in a large, deep saucepan with a lid over a medium heat. Add the onion and sauté for 12–15 minutes, or until soft and golden.
⊙ Add the white wine and mussels and cover. Shake the saucepan to help distribute the heat evenly while holding the lid on firmly. Continue for 7–9 minutes, or until the mussels have opened. Discard any mussels that haven't opened.
⊙ Remove the mussels and place into serving bowls. Leave the broth on the heat and bring to the boil. Stir in remaining ingredients, season with salt and pepper and pour over mussels.
⊙ Serve with fresh crusty bread to soak up the broth.

Parmesan-crusted flathead

Everyone fought over this dish at the photo shoot. It is one of those delectable four-ingredient, five-minute dishes! Serve with wilted spinach and mashed potato or as a snack with home-made wedges and a squeeze of lemon. Serves 2.

2 x 175 g flathead fish fillets, cut into
  5 cm strips
¼ cup plain flour
½ cup milk
light olive oil
3 tablespoons finely grated
  Parmesan

⊙ Lightly dust the fish with flour and season with salt and pepper. Dip in the milk and then coat lightly with Parmesan.
⊙ Heat enough oil to reach about 1 cm up the sides of a thick-based frying pan. Cook the fish for about 2 minutes on each side, or until cooked and golden.
⊙ Serve on a bed of broad beans with chilli and mint (see page 113).

Eggs are a great option for a fast meal. Tasty and filling, they're the ultimate versatile food.

Eggs are packed with great nutrition including protein, vitamins A, D, E, and B group, as well as minerals, iron, phosphorus and zinc. Plus, we now know that eggs contain many nutrients that actually protect against illness. They're pretty low in saturated fat, making them a healthy fast food, and there are 76 calories per medium-sized egg. If you are really particular, you can remove the yolk, which makes the egg almost fat free.

In my opinion, organic or farm-grown eggs taste the best.

eggs

Hard-boiled eggs

Hard-boiled eggs have a solid yolk which is cooked to a pale butter yellow. They are perfect for sandwiches and salads and dishes where the yolk is required for taste, texture or colour (eg, curried egg). Or, eat them whole.

To hard-boil eggs, gently lower the eggs into boiling water and cook for 12 minutes. Drain and rinse them under cold water to stop them from cooking further.

NOTE: Eggs cook best when they're at room temperature.

Soft-boiled eggs

Soft-boiled eggs have a runny yolk that retains its dark, glossy orange-yellow colour. They are great with toast for breakfast, or for using over rice dishes such as fried rice or nasi goreng.

To soft-boil eggs, reduce the heat to a simmer after you have lowered the eggs into the boiling water. Cook for 5 minutes, then drain and rinse them under cold water.

Basic omelette

The fresher the eggs, the lighter the omelette. You can make sweet omelettes too. Take away the salt and pepper and add chocolate flakes, crushed nuts, vanilla or fruit and finish with a dusting of icing sugar. I like to leave one side of the omelette slightly moist as this prevents it from becoming 'dry' inside. Makes an omelette for 1.

2–3 eggs, at room temperature
1/2 an eggshell water
1/2 tablespoon butter

NOTE: For a herby alternative, sprinkle a tablespoon of chopped fine herbs such as chervil, tarragon, parsley and chives over your omelette just before serving.

Add the water to the eggs and beat lightly with a fork. Season with salt and pepper.

Melt the butter in a medium-sized frying pan. When the foam in the beaten egg subsides, transfer the eggs to the pan and cook over medium heat, lifting the side of the omelette to let the uncooked egg run out to the edges.

When the omelette is seconds away from being set, gently fold it in half and serve.

hard- and soft-boiled eggs

Spanish fried eggs

Jason's scrambled eggs

A gorgeous lower-fat option. Not only have I substituted cream, a saturated fat, with olive oil, a more unsaturated fat, but these eggs taste good too. Serves 2

2 eggs
2 tablespoons extra virgin olive oil
a pinch salt
a pinch ground pepper, preferably
  white pepper
a pinch ground nutmeg
1/2 teaspoon butter

Using a fork, lightly beat the eggs, oil and seasoning together in a bowl.

Melt the butter in a non-stick frying pan over medium to low heat. Pour in the eggs, allowing them to partially set before using a wooden spoon to pull them back gently as you tilt the pan. Repeat the process for a couple of minutes, or until they are almost set. Then remove the eggs from the pan straightaway to prevent further cooking and drying out.

Serve immediately on toasted Turkish bread.

Spanish fried eggs

This is Sunday brekky in bed! Serves 2

2 tomatoes, finely diced
1 small Spanish onion, chopped finely
1 red chilli, finely chopped
1 1/2 tablespoons olive oil
2 eggs
2 slices wood-fired bread (or normal
  bread, but the wood-fired is tastier!)

To make the salsa, mix together the tomato, onion, chilli and 1 tablespoon of the olive oil. Season with salt and pepper.

Heat the remaining olive oil in a non-stick frying pan and fry the eggs until cooked to your liking. Remove from the pan.

Add the slices of bread to the pan and cook until lightly toasted.

Serve the eggs on the toast and sprinkle with salsa.

Mixed mushroom, rosemary and Gruyère clafoutis

Clafoutis is traditionally a French dessert, but here's a savoury version, which looks like an upside-down omelette. You could add whatever vegetables you have available. Serves 2

3 eggs, lightly beaten
1 1/2 cups milk
1/2 cup flour
1 tablespoon olive oil
300 g small mixed mushrooms
1 clove garlic, thinly sliced
1 teaspoon rosemary, finely chopped
2/3 cup grated Gruyère cheese
truffle oil (optional)

Preheat the oven to 200°C.

Beat the eggs and milk together and then beat in the flour until it is the consistency of a thin batter. Season with salt and pepper and set aside.

Heat the oil in an ovenproof frying pan, then add the mushrooms and garlic. Cook for 3 minutes or until browned. (Any juices that have been released should have evaporated.) Stir in the rosemary.

Stir the Gruyère through the batter and pour it over the mushrooms. Bake for 30 minutes. Serve with a green salad and drizzle with truffle oil if desired.

Semi-dried tomato, asparagus and Gruyère frittata

If you want small individual frittatas instead of one big one, pour the mixture into a muffin tin lined with strips of greaseproof paper, top with cheese and grill as directed below. They're great for straight-out-of-the-fridge snacks. You can also use this recipe for a quiche filling — just pour it into a pie-crust and bake as directed below. Serves 2, or makes 3–4 mini frittatas.

8 spears asparagus, trimmed and
  roughly chopped
¼ cup water
8 eggs
¼ cup grated Parmesan (50 g)
¼ cup basil leaves, torn
4 semi-dried tomatoes, roughly
  chopped
1 tablespoon olive oil
¼ cup grated Gruyère cheese (50 g)

NOTE: To roast your own tomatoes,
see page 56.

Put the asparagus in a microwave-proof dish with the water and cover with cling wrap. Cook in the microwave on high for 60 seconds. Remove and drain. You could also steam the asparagus for 3 minutes or blanch it in an inch of boiling water.

Combine the eggs, salt and pepper, Parmesan and half the basil in a small bowl. Beat the mixture lightly with a fork. Add the asparagus and tomatoes.

Preheat the griller.

Heat the oil in a medium-sized frying pan. Pour in the egg mixture and swirl it so that the pan is covered. Cook over medium heat, loosening the sides occasionally, for about 8 minutes, or until nearly set.

Sprinkle the frittata with the Gruyère and place it under the grill for a couple of minutes, or until golden and puffy. Garnish with the remaining basil.

Cheat's omelette

As peculiar as it sounds, this works! This omelette comes out of the bag looking like an 'egg sausage'. Slice it and serve on thick buttered toast, or slice it cold and throw it into an iceberg lettuce salad with mayo. Serves 1.

2 eggs
1 tablespoon diced capsicum
1 spring onion, sliced
1 slice ham, diced
2 tablespoons shredded cheese

Put a large pot of water on to boil.

In a bowl, beat the eggs and combine them with the capsicum, spring onion, ham and cheese. Season with salt and pepper.

Place the mixture in a large freezer bag and tie the bag. Shake well, then drop the bag into the boiling water. Keep boiling for about three minutes, or until the egg has set. Remove the omelette from the bag and serve immediately.

cheat's omelette

omelette with goat's cheese,
rocket and toasted almonds

Spanish tortilla with green olives

I recently prepared this dish with totally organic ingredients. They gave it a distinct flavour edge.
Serves 2–4.

½ cup olive oil
4 large potatoes (500 g), cut into
  2 mm slices (use Desiree potatoes
  if you can)
1 large onion, roughly sliced
1 clove garlic, crushed
6 eggs
1 tablespoon fresh thyme
10 green olives, seeds removed and
  finely chopped

Heat the oil in a heavy, non-stick pan over medium heat. When the oil is hot, reduce the temperature to low and add the potatoes, onion and garlic. Cook, stirring frequently, for 15–20 minutes or until the potatoes are tender.

Beat the eggs in a large bowl with salt, pepper and fresh thyme. Using a slotted spoon, transfer the potatoes, onion and garlic to the egg mixture. Add the olives. Pour any excess oil off the pan and reserve it. Scrape any burnt bits from the bottom of the pan and discard.

Return the pan to the heat and add 2 tablespoons of the reserved oil. Pour in the potato and egg mixture and arrange the potatoes and onions in an even layer. Cook for about 5 minutes, shaking the pan occasionally, or until the base is set.

Loosen the tortilla with a spatula, and place a large plate over the pan. Invert the tortilla onto the plate and return the pan to the heat. Add a tablespoon of the reserved oil to the pan and slide the tortilla back onto it, uncooked side down. Push the sides down with a spatula and cook for 3–5 minutes.

Remove the tortilla from the pan and allow to cool for 10 minutes before serving.

Omelette with goat's cheese, rocket and toasted almonds

Best served piping hot straight from the pan. Makes an omelette for 1.

1 quantity basic omelette (see
  page 96)
30 g goat's cheese, crumbled
½ cup rocket
2 tablespoons toasted almonds,
  roughly chopped

Cook the omelette as directed on page 96. When it is nearly set, sprinkle the goat's cheese and rocket over it. Cook for a few seconds more, then fold it in half and scatter the almonds over the top. Serve.

It's all about variety. Quite often I find myself ordering several side dishes instead of a main so I can sample a bit of everything. Accompaniments can be eaten as a meal in themselves or added to various meats, rice dishes and other basics to create little masterpieces.

It's all about freshness. 'Bit on the side' shows off our fresh Australian produce and proves you can do a lot with whatever happens to be in season.

It's all about little meals. Graze – have small meals more often! It's better for your weight and your heart, and keeps your energy and glycogen levels up.

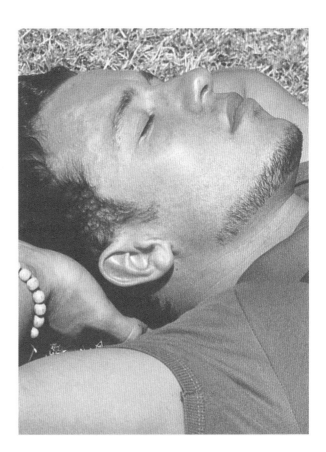

bit on the side

Zucchini with squash and hazelnuts

A delicious vegetable side dish. If you don't have both zucchini and squash, you can use one or the other. Serves 4.

250 g zucchini

250 g squash

2 tablespoons olive oil

1/2 cup hazelnuts, roughly chopped

Cut the zucchini into 5 cm lengths and quarter the squash.

Bring a medium-sized saucepan of salted water to the boil, then add the zucchini and/or squash and cook for 3–4 minutes. Drain and set aside.

Heat the oil in a frying pan, add the hazelnuts and season well with salt and pepper. Fry for about 5 minutes, or until golden. Add the zucchini and/or squash and stir until combined and warmed through. Serve.

Lentils with spinach and egg

This is both a salad and a side dish. It's great with chicken poached with tarragon (see page 63). Serves 4 as an accompaniment.

3 tablespoons olive oil

2 cloves garlic, sliced

400 g tinned lentils

150 g baby spinach leaves

2 hard-boiled eggs, quartered (see page 96)

Heat the olive oil in a large frying pan. Add the garlic and cook until browned, making sure it doesn't burn.

Add the lentils and baby spinach and cook until the lentils are warmed through and the spinach has wilted.

Remove from the heat and add the eggs, then season with salt and pepper and serve.

Broccoli with almonds and anchovies

Greens are sensational for their nutrition, colour and taste. This dish gives ordinary broccoli a real kick! Serves 4–6 as an accompaniment.

500 g broccoli, cut into florets

2 tablespoons olive oil

1/3 cup almonds, chopped

5 anchovy fillets

pepper

Bring a pot of salted water to the boil. Add the broccoli and cook for 4 minutes. Drain well and set aside.

Heat the oil in a frying pan. Add the almonds, anchovies and a generous grinding of pepper. Stirring with a wooden spoon, cook for 5–6 minutes, or until the anchovies break up and the almonds turn golden.

Add the broccoli and cook until warmed through. Serve.

broccoli with almonds and anchovies

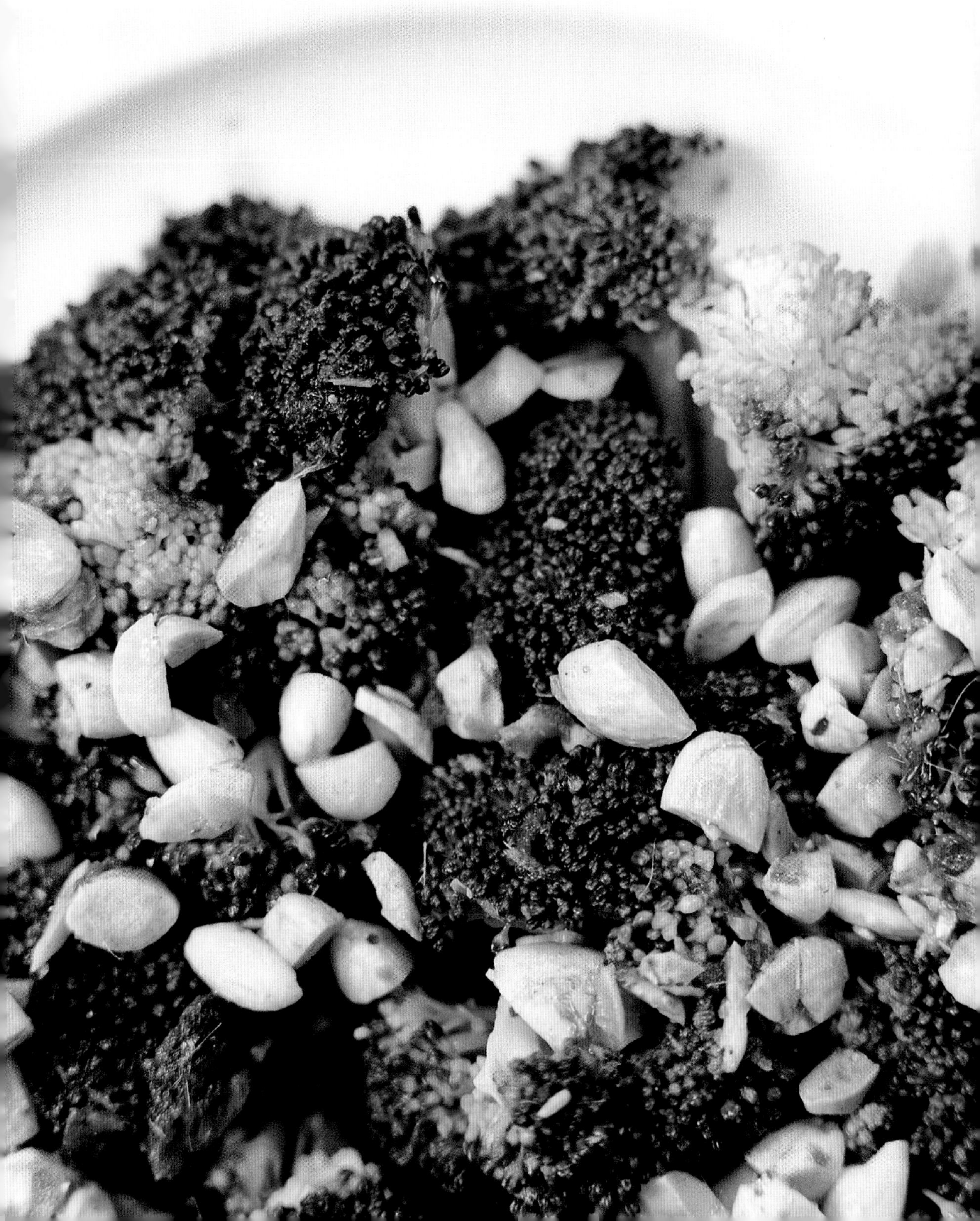

asparagus and Parmesan

Asparagus and Parmesan

Serves 6 as an accompaniment.

2 bunches asparagus (about 24
  spears), woody ends removed
1/3 cup grated Parmesan
2 tablespoons olive oil

Bring a large pot of salted water to the boil. Add the asparagus and cook for 7 minutes (cooking time will vary according to the thickness of the asparagus). Drain and set aside.

Preheat the griller. Place the asparagus on a baking tray, scatter the Parmesan over the top and drizzle with olive oil. Season with salt and pepper and grill for 4–5 minutes, or until golden. Serve.

Pumpkin roasted with fennel seeds and chilli

I use a whole pumpkin for this recipe, even though you probably only need about one-third for two serves. You can use the rest of the pumpkin in soup, a purée or perhaps a Turkish bread pizza. It is delicious used in roast pumpkin, basil and fennel risotto (see page 17). Serves 8 as an accompaniment.

1 kg butternut pumpkin
2 tablespoons olive oil
1 tablespoon fennel seeds
1/2 teaspoon chilli flakes

Preheat the oven to 200°C.

Split your pumpkin into quarters and remove the seeds with a spoon. Leave the skin on, as it has a tendency to crisp up and taste a little like roasted chestnuts when roasted.

Place the quarters on an oven tray that has been lined with greaseproof paper. Douse with the oil, salt, pepper, fennel and chilli seeds, and rub them into the pumpkin flesh.

Roast for about 40 minutes, turning a couple of times during the roasting process to get a lovely, even golden glaze on the surface of the pumpkin.

The pumpkin is ready if you can push a knife or skewer into the flesh without any resistance.

Sautéed mushrooms with butter and garlic

A Sunday morning favourite. Serves 2.

400 g mixed mushrooms (a selection
   of oyster, Swiss brown and
   chestnut mushrooms is lovely), cut
   into rough chunks
1 tablespoon olive oil
1 tablespoon butter
2 cloves garlic, sliced
1 teaspoon of mixed dried herbs
   (marjoram, thyme, rosemary and
   sage, for example)
a squeeze lemon juice
¼ cup chicken stock

Heat the oil and butter in a frying pan. Add the garlic and cook until golden. Add the mushrooms and herbs and cook for 5–6 minutes, or until the mushrooms are lightly browned.

Add the lemon juice and chicken stock and cook until the stock is reduced by half. Season with salt and pepper and serve.

Carrots with honey and cider

Serves 4 as an accompaniment.

3 large carrots, peeled and cut into
   3 cm chunks
1½ tablespoons cider vinegar
1 tablespoon honey
1 tablespoon extra virgin olive oil

Place the carrots in a saucepan and pour in enough water to just cover them. Add the cider vinegar, honey and olive oil. Bring to a simmer. Season with salt and pepper and cook, uncovered, for 15 minutes or until the carrots are tender and the liquid has reduced to about 2 cm in the bottom of the pan. Serve.

Brussels sprouts with walnuts

Serves 4–6 as an accompaniment.

500 g brussels sprouts
1 tablespoons olive oil
1 tablespoon butter
⅓ cup walnuts, roughly chopped
1 teaspoon rosemary, chopped
a squeeze lemon juice

Remove the outer leaves of the brussels sprouts, and cut a criss-cross pattern in the bases. Halve them if they are large.

Bring a pot of salted water to the boil. Add the sprouts and cook for 10 minutes. Drain well and set aside.

Heat the oil and butter in a thick-based frying pan. Add the walnuts and rosemary and cook for 4–5 minutes over medium heat until the nuts are golden. Add the sprouts and cook until they are warmed through. Season with salt and pepper and toss the lemon juice through. Serve immediately.

brussels sprouts with almonds

corn on the cob with five-spice

Broad beans with chilli and mint

Serves 4 as an accompaniment, or as a bed for meat or fish.

500 g frozen broad beans
2 tablespoons olive oil
1/2 teaspoon chilli flakes
10 mint leaves, shredded
Parmesan, shaved

NOTE: 500 g of broad beans becomes 300 g when peeled. If broad beans are unavailable, substitute them with 300 g peas.

Bring a pot of salted water to the boil. Add the broad beans and cook for 3–4 minutes. Drain and rinse the beans under cold water, then peel them.

Heat the oil in a frying pan. Add the chilli and cook for 30 seconds. Add the peeled beans and cook until warmed through, then add the mint and toss. Season with salt and pepper and scatter with shaved Parmesan if desired. Serve.

Corn on the cob with five-spice

Serves 2.

2 corn cobs, husks still intact
2 tablespoons olive oil
1/2 teaspoon five-spice powder
cracked pepper

Pull back the husks of the corn. Remove the silky threads, then replace the leaves.

Soak the corn in warm water for 30 minutes. Drain.

In a small bowl, combine the oil and five-spice. Pull back the husks again and brush the oil and five-spice over the corn.

Heat a chargrill pan. Cook the corn on high heat for 20–25 minutes, turning occasionally. Drizzle with any remaining oil and season with cracked pepper. Serve.

Caramelised witlof with Parmesan

Mouth-watering with Tuscan-style spatchcock (see page 64). Serves 4 as an accompaniment.

2 tablespoons butter
400 g witlof, halved, base trimmed
2 tablespoons shaved Parmesan
balsamic vinegar

Melt the butter in a thick-based frying pan. Season the witlof with salt and pepper and place in the pan, cut side down.

Cover the pan with baking paper (you can cut it to fit) and cook on medium heat. The paper will allow the witlof to steam as it caramelises. Cook for 15–20 minutes until the witlof is soft and golden, turning it after about 10 minutes. Sprinkle with the Parmesan and drizzle with balsamic vinegar. Serve.

Cabbage braised with apples and white wine

Great with pan-fried cod, braised beef, pork sausages and anything gamey. It is my favourite accompaniment for snapper in a bag (see page 86). Serves 4 as an accompaniment.

3 tablespoons olive oil
1 onion, finely sliced
200 g bacon, chopped (get speck if possible)
1 kg cabbage, sliced
½ cup white wine
2 apples, peeled and grated thickly (I prefer Golden Delicious)

○ Heat the oil in a large, thick-based frying pan. Add the onions and cook until soft and translucent, then add the bacon and cook until golden.
○ Add the sliced cabbage and cook until it has wilted. Add the white wine and apple and cook over low heat, covered, for 45–60 minutes. Season well with salt and pepper and serve.

Tomato, white bean and silver beet gratin

Serves 4 as an accompaniment.

1 tablespoon olive oil
1 onion, sliced
2 cloves garlic, crushed
1 bunch silver beet (about 550 g), white stem removed, roughly chopped
2 vine-ripened tomatoes, roughly chopped
400 g tinned cannellini beans, drained and rinsed
½ tablespoon lemon juice
4 sprigs fresh thyme
1 cup fresh breadcrumbs
2 tablespoons chopped parsley
2 tablespoons grated Parmesan

○ Heat the oil in a frying pan, add the onion and cook until soft. Add the garlic and cook for a further 30 seconds. Add the silver beet and cook until it has wilted and excess water has evaporated. Add the tomatoes and cook, stirring, for 5 minutes.
○ Stir the beans, lemon juice and thyme through the beet and tomatoes and pour the mixture into a medium-sized ovenproof dish.
○ In a small bowl, combine the breadcrumbs, Parmesan and parsley. Sprinkle over the top of the beet mixture and bake for 20 minutes, or until the breadcrumbs are golden.

cabbage braised with apples
and white wine

Nana Goodman's rissolia

Creamed silver beet

Serves 4 as an accompaniment.

1 large bunch silver beet
1 tablespoon butter
a pinch nutmeg

Bring a large saucepan of salted water to the boil. Add the silver beet and cook for 8–20 minutes, or until it nearly falls apart between your fingers. Drain, letting drops of water cling to the leaves.

Transfer to a blender or food processor and add the butter. Purée till smooth and season with nutmeg, salt and pepper. Serve.

Nana Goodman's rissolia

This is a Russian-style salad that my Nana Goodman often makes for our family. We eat it for lunch or dinner, and sometimes as an accompaniment to a selection of cold meats or other little salads. The best thing about this salad is that Nana always gives us some to take home, and it's even tastier the next day. This is a luscious, vibrant salad best served chilled. This recipe uses tinned salmon, but you can poach your own if you like. Serves 4–6 as an accompaniment.

For the salad:
6 waxy potatoes, such as Kipfler or
   pink-eye varieties, boiled till firm
   but cooked through
2 large apples
4 hard-boiled eggs
415 g tinned salmon
425 g tinned baby beets or sliced
   beetroot
1 Lebanese cucumber, cut into 1 cm
   chunks
1 onion, finely chopped
100 g ham, finely diced

For the dressing:
1/4 cup thickened light cream
2/3 cup light sour cream
1 teaspoon salt
2 teaspoons sugar
2 teaspoons Dijon mustard
pepper to taste
2 tablespoons chopped parsley

Chop the potato, apples, eggs, beetroot and salmon into bit-size chunks.

Mix all the salad ingredients together in a bowl.

In another bowl, combine the dressing ingredients. Pour them over the salad and toss through.

Allow the salad to sit overnight in the fridge, covered, if you can resist the temptation that long.

Snacking used to be a dirty word, but not any more. Grazing – or eating more small-portion meals, more often – is actually thought to be the best way to keep healthy and maintain your weight – provided the snacks are balanced!

Most of these snacks can be made in less than 10 minutes and will keep you going for a few hours. I have used some commercial products to lessen the preparation time involved. You can keep the basics for most snacks in your freezer or cupboard, so they are there whenever the mood takes you. Here is a list of ingredients to keep handy:
• frozen puff pastry
• un-sliced bread
• sliced bread or rolls
• tomato paste and tomato sauce
• flour
• salt
• cheese
• baking powder
• olive oil

Add a few fresh ingredients to these basics and you can make almost anything small and sassy!

sassy snacks

Potted veal pies

I'm very fond of the potted pie. If starting from scratch, it could take a couple of hours, but it's very quick if you can use leftover stewed meat such as lamb shanks. This recipe makes 4–6 small pies, but you could also make one large one.

¼ cup olive oil
1 large onion, finely sliced
1 kg veal shoulder or leg meat, bone, skin and excess fat removed, cut into 2 cm cubes
80 g plain flour
4 cups chicken stock
¼ teaspoon nutmeg
2 tablespoons chopped parsley
¼ cup cream

○ In a thick-based pan, sweat (do not brown) the onions in the olive oil till tender. Add the meat and sweat it until the meat has changed colour but not browned. Sift in flour and mix evenly. Cook without browning for a few minutes.
○ Slowly add the chicken stock. Season to taste with pepper and the nutmeg. Cover the pan with a piece of greaseproof paper and braise for about 1 hour 40 minutes, stirring occasionally. The meat is ready when it is tender and a skewer can easily be pushed into it. Add the parsley and cream. Season to taste with salt.
○ Preheat the oven to 220°C. Cut discs of pastry to fit the top of your 'pots'. (These need to be heatproof; I've chosen a sturdy coffee mug.) Fill the pots with the braised veal, leaving about 0.5 cm from the top free. Brush the rim of the pot with water and cover with the pastry. Puncture the pastry a few times with a knife to allow the pie a vent as it's cooking.
○ Cook in the oven for 12–15 minutes, or until the pastry has turned a golden brown. Allow to stand for 2 minutes before serving.

Fresh herb bread

This bread is great for a barbecue, and it will keep for a few weeks if wrapped in foil and plastic wrap and frozen. Use any herbs you may have in the fridge, or add 2 teaspoons of dried herbs if fresh are unavailable. You can also keep the herb and butter mixture in the freezer for up to a month. Makes 6–8 pieces.

1 medium-sized baguette
120 g soft butter
1 clove garlic, crushed
2 tablespoons chopped parsley
1 teaspoon chopped thyme
2 teaspoons chopped oregano
a pinch salt
2–3 tablespoons grated Parmesan

○ Preheat the oven to 200°C.
○ Slice the baguette on the diagonal into 2–3 cm slices, making sure you don't slice right through to the bottom.
○ Combine the butter, garlic, herbs, salt and Parmesan in a small bowl and mix them together. Generously butter both sides of the bread slices.
○ Wrap the baguette in foil and bake for 15 minutes. For a crusty version, unwrap the bread after 10 minutes and bake on a tray for the final 5 minutes.

potted veal pies

Turkish bread pizza

Here's a quick pizza idea. There is so much available in delicatessens and even supermarkets these days that you can use for the toppings. Try tapenade, roasted peppers or pesto. Just like takeaway pizza, this is fantastic eaten cold in the morning after a big night out! Makes 2 pizzas.

1 Turkish bread, sliced in half lengthwise

2 tablespoons extra virgin olive oil

1/2 clove garlic

6–8 artichokes (or one small 375 g jar)

12 cherry tomatoes, halved

125 g marinated goat's milk Feta (about 1/2 cup)

5 slices prosciutto, torn into large pieces

1 tablespoon oregano leaves

○ Preheat the oven to 220°C.

○ Brush some of the oil over the cut sides of the bread. Place the bread slices in the oven and cook on both sides until crisp. Remove from the oven and rub the cut edge of the garlic over the oiled surfaces. Discard the garlic piece.

○ Arrange the artichokes, tomatoes, Feta and prosciutto pieces on the bread. Season with salt, pepper and oregano and drizzle with the remaining olive oil. Bake for 10–15 minutes, or until crisp.

Smoked chicken and avocado pancakes

These are my favourite, but other delicious combinations include salsa and fried egg pancakes and cucumber, sour cream and smoked salmon pancakes. Makes 6 pancakes.

1 egg

1/2 cup milk

2 tablespoons olive oil

1/3 cup plain flour

1 teaspoon baking powder

a pinch salt

freshly ground black pepper

butter for cooking

2 smoked chicken breasts, shredded

1 small avocado, sliced

1/3 cup whole egg mayonnaise

juice of half a lemon

cracked pepper

1 1/2 cups rocket

○ Using a fork, whisk the egg, milk and olive oil until well combined.

○ In another bowl, sift the flour, baking powder, salt and pepper. Then gradually pour in the egg mixture, beating lightly with a whisk until smooth. Set aside to rest for 30 minutes.

○ Heat a non-stick frying pan with a little butter over medium heat. When the foam from the eggs has subsided drop approximately 3 heaped tablespoons of pancake batter into the pan to form one pancake. Cook until bubbles appear on the top of the pancake. Use a spatula to flip the pancake and cook until golden on the other side.

○ Keep warm in low heat in the oven while cooking the remaining pancakes.

○ Mix together the chicken pieces, avocado, mayonnaise, lemon and pepper. Place the avocado and chicken mixture on top of the pancakes. Top with the rocket and serve.

smoked chicken and
avocado pancakes

corned beef and cabbage sandwich

Jase's favourite sambo: corned beef and cabbage

By slicing a foot-long, unsliced loaf of bread lengthwise you get one big sambo that makes 3 servings. Another yummy combination is tuna, mayo, Spanish onion, iceberg lettuce and S&P sauce.

1 loaf unsliced bread
wholegrain mustard to spread
4 large slices leftover corned beef
leftover braised cabbage with apple
    and white wine (see page 114), or
    use ½ cup cabbage
good quality aged cheddar cheese
a knob butter

NOTE: For a quick version of the cabbage mixture, throw ½ cup of cabbage, 3 tablespoons of grated apple and 1 tablespoon of white wine into a microwave dish and microwave on high for 3 minutes.

⊙ Slice the bread lengthwise into 6 thick slices. Spread mustard over the bread and pile the corned beef, cabbage and cheese on top.

⊙ Melt the butter in a large, thick-based frying pan. Fry both sides of the sandwich over medium heat until golden and the cheese has melted. A tip from my friend Tezza: after frying the bread, fry a slice of cheese on the bread, then flip and fry one onto the other side, before adding any sandwich fillings. Makes for an over-indulgent, ultra crispy, triple cheesy flavour sensation!

Fried fresh ricotta and asparagus wraps

Here's a great little number to tempt the taste buds. This wrap also doubles as finger food – just slice the roll into 2 cm lengths and douse in a little extra virgin olive oil. Serves 2.

3 anchovy fillets
½ clove garlic
120 g fresh ricotta
3 tablespoons olive oil
1 piece of flat bread, lavash or a
    flour tortilla
4–6 spears asparagus, blanched until
    tender, then refreshed under cold
    running water and dried well

⊙ Finely chop the anchovies and garlic together till you've almost created a paste. Throw into a bowl along with the ricotta and 1 tablespoon of the olive oil. Season with salt and pepper and mix well.

⊙ Spread the mixture evenly over the flat bread, leaving a 3 cm strip along the longer side of the bread uncovered. Place the asparagus down the centre of the ricotta mixture, then roll the bread up firmly.

⊙ Heat the remaining olive oil in a pan over medium heat. Place the roll into the pan, flap down. Turn every 20–30 seconds until you get an even golden colour.

⊙ To serve just cut in half. This one is definitely best eaten straight out of the pan.

Prawn and avocado baguette

I know prawns aren't cheap, but when I really feel like indulging, I can't go past a feed of prawns and avocados all wrapped up in a chewy baguette. Adding chopped chives or basil to the mix is a nice touch, too. Serves 4.

1 baguette
500 g prawns, cooked and peeled
   (will leave you with about 250 g
   meat)
1 small, ripe avocado, peeled,
   seeded and cut into 1 cm chunks
2 heaped tablespoons whole egg
   mayonnaise
juice of half a lime (or 1 teaspoon
   lemon juice)

◦ Run a bread knife lengthwise down the side of the baguette, opening it up, then use your fingers to hollow it out. (Freeze the fresh bread taken from inside – it makes wicked breadcrumbs.)
◦ Mix the mayonnaise with the lime juice and season with salt and freshly ground black pepper. Fold the cooked prawns and avocado through, then stuff the mixture into the hollowed out baguette.
◦ Slice into portions as desired. Wrapped in cling film, this will keep in the fridge for a few hours, but is definitely best served fresh.

Tomato and Parmesan tart

Frozen puff pastry makes this a very quick snack! Scatter basil over it for colour. For bite-size tarts, cut the pastry before transferring it to the hot tray and place a slice of tomato and scattered cheese on each square. Bake as directed below. Serves 1, or makes 9 bite-size tarts.

1 sheet shop-bought puff pastry
1 tomato, sliced
4–6 tablespoons grated Parmesan
cracked black pepper

◦ Preheat the oven to 220°C.
◦ Carefully remove one of the trays while the oven is heating. Put the pastry on a piece of greaseproof paper on the tray. Place the sliced tomato over it and scatter the Parmesan across the top. Season with pepper and bake for 15 minutes or until golden. Serve.

tomato and Parmesan tart

Tim tam bomb

Be selfish! Find a quiet place, your favourite chair, and hook into a packet of Tim Tams. This is the most tantalising sweet treat – and without any preparation.

⊚ Bite two corners off opposite ends of your Tim Tam. Dunk it into a mug of hot chocolate or coffee and suck the liquid through the opposite end like a straw. It's heaven!

Always order dessert. I do! But I try to go easy on the portion size. How often can you find small desserts? It's tricky, so I have included a few recipes here which serve one or two people instead of a whole army (because let's be honest – if you make a cake that serves eight and there are only two of you, you eventually eat it all anyway, right!).

I also love to try really different things when it comes to desserts, and I love fresh fruit. Some of these sweet things are old favourites (ginger crunch, page 137) and some will bring a new twist to dessert (lychees with Frangelico, page 134), but all of them are delicious and easy.

short & sweet

Hazelnut crème caramel

Makes 6.

125 g roasted hazelnuts

1 cup milk

1¾ cups cream

1½ cups caster sugar

¼ cup water

2 tablespoons extra water

4 egg yolks and 2 eggs

juice of a couple of limes (optional)

Frangelico (optional)

○ Preheat the oven to 200°C.

○ On a lined tray, roast the hazelnuts until browned. Chop and place them in a saucepan along with the milk and cream. Heat until nearly boiling, then set the pan aside for at least 30 minutes. Strain to remove the hazelnuts. Reduce the oven heat to 140°C.

○ For the caramel, place ¾ cup of the caster sugar in a medium-sized saucepan with the water. Stir over low heat until the sugar has dissolved. Bring to the boil and cook for 6–7 minutes, or until the syrup turns a deep golden colour. Quickly add the extra water to arrest the cooking. Pour into 6 x 200 ml moulds.

○ In a bowl, beat the egg yolks, eggs and remaining caster sugar until creamy. Gradually add the infused milk and cream mixture. Pour over the caramel in the moulds and skim off any bubbles.

○ Place the moulds in a deep-sided baking tin with enough hot water in it to come halfway up the sides of the moulds. Bake for 45–60 minutes. It will be ready when there is the slightest wobble to the centre when shaken. Cool for at least 4 hours.

○ To serve, run a knife around the edge of each mould, then turn them out onto a plate and sprinkle with lime juice and Frangelico if desired.

Almond rice pudding

This pudding is very light and airy, and you can add any fruit you like to vary the taste. Stewed rhubarb and apples are favourites of mine. I like to make this dessert when I'm cooking for a big dinner party, as you can whip it up the night before and it's ready to go! Serves 4.

1⅓ cups milk

⅙ cup caster sugar

a pinch salt

1 vanilla bean, split and seeds scraped out, or 1 teaspoon vanilla essence

¼ cup uncooked medium grain rice

⅓ cup cream

a couple drops almond essence

1 big handful flaked almonds (30 g), toasted

2 oranges, peeled and segmented

○ Bring the milk, sugar, salt and vanilla to the boil in a medium-sized saucepan.

○ Stir in the rice, reduce the heat to low and continue stirring regularly for about 10 minutes, or until the rice is completely cooked. Set the saucepan aside and allow to cool.

○ Whip the cream to soft peaks, then add the almond essence. Fold about one-third of the rice through at a time until all is incorporated evenly.

○ Place in the refrigerator for 20 minutes, then scatter the toasted almonds over the chilled pudding and serve.

hazelnut crème caramel

pear tarte tatin

Chocolate tart

The ultimate dessert. Serve with double cream or vanilla-bean ice-cream. If using shop-bought pastry, try to buy large sheets, or join smaller ones by pushing the edges firmly together. Serves 8.

1 sheet sweet shortcrust pastry
320 g cooking chocolate, broken into pieces
120 g butter
3 eggs and 2 egg yolks
1/2 cup sugar
1 tablespoon Cointreau

○ Preheat the oven to 200°C.

○ Line a 22 cm tart tin with the pastry. Trim the edges. Line the pastry with greaseproof paper and cover with dry beans or rice to weigh the pastry down. Bake in the oven for about 10 minutes, then remove the paper and beans or rice and cook for a further 5 minutes until lightly browned. Remove and set aside to cool.

○ Reduce the heat to 160°C. In a pan, gently melt the chocolate and butter over low heat until liquid. Watch carefully to avoid burning.

○ Beat the eggs, egg yolks and sugar until pale and thick. Fold in the chocolate and Cointreau. Pour this filling into the pastry shell in the tart tin and bake for 20–25 minutes or until the filling has set (you'll know it has set if the filling wobbles like jelly when gently shaken). Allow to cool before serving.

Pear tarte tatin

Impressive, beautiful and laughably easy! Five basics and 35 minutes are all it takes. Serves 8.

4–5 pears, ripe and slightly firm (preferably Beurre Bosc)
50 g unsalted butter
100 g caster sugar
1 sheet frozen puff pastry, defrosted
1 egg, beaten

○ Preheat the oven to 220°C.

○ Place the rim of a medium-sized, ovenproof frying pan (about 24 cm in diameter) over the puff pastry and cut to fit, then place the pastry back into the fridge till it's needed.

○ Peel the pears, halve them lengthways and cut each into 6 thick wedges like orange segments. Remove the seeds.

○ Melt the butter in the frying pan. Stir in the sugar and arrange the pears neatly to fill the bottom of the pan. Cook for 10–15 minutes over moderate heat, or until the pears have caramelised and the juices have become thick, dark and syrupy. (Cooking time will depend on the ripeness of the pears – the riper they are the quicker it will be.)

○ Place the pastry over the pears and tuck the edges down the sides. Pierce the centre of the pastry with two knife-holes, then brush the surface with the beaten egg.

○ Place the pan in the oven and cook for 20 minutes, or until the pastry is crisp and golden. Allow to cool for a few minutes, then invert onto a serving plate.

Mega chunky chocolate macadamia nut cookies

When I first met my partner Kylie, I bribed her into dating me by making her these cookies, laced with bits of Cherry Ripe, Snickers and M&M's. Not a great diet option – but it worked! This recipe can also be made as a slice – press the mixture into a flat, rectangular tin that is lined with greaseproof paper. Cook for an extra few minutes and cut into diagonal slices before totally cool. Makes 12–16 big cookies.

2½ cups plain flour

1 teaspoon baking soda

½ teaspoon baking powder

a pinch salt

200 g unsalted butter, at room
   temperature

¾ cup granulated sugar

1 cup light brown sugar

2 large eggs

1 teaspoon vanilla extract

300 g dark chocolate, broken into
   small chunks

300 g white chocolate, broken into
   small chunks

1 cup roasted macadamia nuts
   (125 g), roughly chopped

○ Preheat the oven to 180°C.

○ In a medium-sized bowl combine the flour, baking soda, baking powder and salt.

○ In a separate bowl cream the butter and white and brown sugar until light and fluffy. Beat the eggs in one at a time, then add the vanilla and fold in the flour. Stir in the chocolate pieces and chopped macadamia nuts.

○ Spoon heaped tablespoons of mixture onto a baking tray covered with baking paper, allowing room for spreading. Bake for 20–25 minutes, or until just golden. Cool on wire racks before serving.

Lychees with Frangelico

How easy is this dessert! I serve it in summer in tall, heavy-based glasses. Use Frangelico to taste (just remember a standard nip is 30 ml). Serves 2–3.

1 tin lychees in light syrup, or about
   6 fresh lychees per glass

Frangelico to taste

lime wedges (1 per glass)

○ Drain the lychees, reserving the syrup.

○ Place them on a plate and whack them in the freezer for a couple of hours until frozen.

○ Place the lychees in a glass and drizzle over a bit of the reserved syrup and some Frangelico.

○ Serve with a lime wedge and a squeeze of lime juice, if desired.

mega chunky chocolate
macadamia nut cookies

rhubarb and raspberry crumble

Rhubarb and raspberry crumble

Another handy timesaver – this can be made the night before. Place it in a hot oven 15 minutes before you serve, then take it straight to the table with a dollop of fresh cream, ice-cream and/or custard. It is also delicious with fresh cold berries and dusted with icing sugar. Serves 2.

1 bunch rhubarb (350 g), trimmed
and cut into 4 cm lengths
1/4 cup caster sugar
1 cup raspberries, fresh or frozen
1/3 cup crushed amaretti biscuits
(80 g)
2 tablespoons brown sugar
1 tablespoon plain flour
50 g butter, melted

○ Preheat the griller.
○ Place the rhubarb and caster sugar in a medium-sized saucepan. Cover and simmer over low heat for 10 minutes or until the rhubarb has softened. Stir in the raspberries and remove from the heat.
○ In a bowl, combine the amaretti biscuits, brown sugar, flour and butter.
○ Spoon the rhubarb into 2 deep heatproof bowls and sprinkle the biscuit mixture over the top. Place under the grill and cook for 2–3 minutes, or until golden.

Grandma Olsen's ginger crunch

I'd been searching for a perfect ginger crunch recipe for years. It is one of those tastes that transport me back to my childhood in an instant. Would you believe it – our photographer, Simon, had a wicked hand-me-down recipe from his Grandma Olsen, and it's a real winner! (See photograph on page 150.) Makes 24 small squares.

For the ginger crunch:
250 g softened butter
1/2 cup caster sugar
2 cups flour
1 teaspoon baking powder
1 tablespoon ground ginger
a pinch salt

For the icing:
1 cup sifted icing sugar
60 g butter
1/4 cup golden syrup
2 teaspoons ginger

○ Preheat the oven to 180°C.
○ Cream the butter and sugar together until white and fluffy. Fold in the sifted flour, baking powder, ground ginger and salt and mix to combine. The mixture should be chunky and sticky. Press the mixture into a greased and lined lamington tin (approximately 20 cm x 30 cm). Bake for 20 minutes or until brown.
○ While the ginger crunch is baking, mix all the icing ingredients together in a small saucepan over moderate heat. Stir until the butter has melted and simmer for 2 minutes.
○ Pour the icing over the top while the ginger crunch is still warm. Slice it into squares before completely cooled.

Stuffed baked peaches

Here's a unique, to-die-for variation of rhubarb crumble. Serves 6.

6 large, ripe peaches

60 g crushed amaretti biscuits

60 g almond meal

50 g brown sugar

1 tablespoon butter, softened

juice of 1 lemon

3–4 tablespoons water

1 tablespoon white sugar

Preheat the oven to 170°C.

Immerse the peaches in boiling water for 10–20 seconds, then plunge them into ice-cold water. Remove the skins, then halve them and remove the stone.

Scoop out about a teaspoon of the flesh from each of the peaches and mix it in a bowl with the crushed amaretti biscuits, almond meal, sugar, butter and a little of the lemon juice to moisten.

Pile the stuffing into the peaches. Place them in a shallow, ovenproof dish along with the water and cover with the white sugar. Bake for about 30 minutes, or until the topping is golden. The peaches will still hold their shape but be very soft if tested with a fork. Serve warm with lightly sweetened whipped cream.

Cherry pancakes

Cherries are amazing, but any fruits that take your fancy can be used for these great pancakes. Berries are especially good – blueberries, raspberries, strawberries – but even bananas or stewed apples work. Makes 6–8 pancakes.

1 cup flour

2 teaspoons baking powder

a pinch salt

2 tablespoons caster sugar

2 eggs, separated

1/2 teaspoon vanilla

1 cup milk

1 cup cherries (150 g), pitted and
  roughly chopped

a knob butter

Sift the flour, baking powder and salt into a bowl. Mix in 1 tablespoon of the sugar.

In another bowl, mix together the egg yolks, vanilla and milk.

Whisk the egg whites and the remaining tablespoon of caster sugar until firm.

Make a well in the dry ingredients and pour in the milk mixture. Mix gradually to combine. Then gently fold in the egg whites and cherries.

Melt the butter in a frying pan and add ladlefuls of mixture. Fry each pancake until bubbles appear, then turn and cook on the other side until golden. To serve, dust with icing sugar and top with fresh cherries, ice-cream and cream if desired.

cherry pancakes

banana and sour cream muffins

Banana and sour cream muffins

For a lower-fat option add nuts or dried fruit instead of sour cream, and to make it more wicked, add some lemon juice to a few tablespoons of icing sugar and drizzle over the top. Makes 6 large muffins.

2 cups flour
¾ teaspoon baking powder
1 teaspoon baking soda
¾ cup caster sugar
2 large ripe bananas, mashed
2 tablespoons sour cream
2 large eggs, lightly beaten
zest of half a lemon
1 teaspoon vanilla essence
120 g butter, melted

Preheat the oven to 200°C.

Sift the flour, baking powder, baking soda and sugar into a large bowl. Make a well in the middle.

In another bowl, mix together the bananas, sour cream, eggs, lemon zest and vanilla essence. Pour this into the well in the dry ingredients, along with the melted butter. Stir until just combined. The mixture should still be lumpy.

Spoon into a greased 6-hole muffin tin. Bake for 20–25 minutes, or until golden.

Gianni's zabaglione

Gianni, a Sicilian, is a great friend of mine and the most amazing untrained cook I know. His marzipan is the best on the planet and his Italian biscuits are heavenly. Zabaglione is a creamy mousse-like, melt-in-the-mouth dessert topping. If you don't want to use berries, the zabaglione is also beautiful over poached stone fruit like peaches, nectarines, apricots. It's pure heaven. Serves 2.

4 egg yokes
4 tablespoons castor sugar
120 ml Marsala
400 g fresh berries

NOTE: Marsala is a sweet, dark, fortified wine from Italy. If you can't get hold of it, you could also use 120 ml Galliano.

Wash and pick through the berries, discarding any bruised or rotten ones. Pour half of the Marsala over the berries, and allow the mixture to sit for a few minutes. (Don't refrigerate.)

Meanwhile, bring a large saucepan of water to simmer, and place a bowl above it. In the bowl, beat the sugar, yokes and remaining Marsala with a whisk for 12–15 minutes, or until they have tripled in volume. The trick here is to constantly whisk, beating air into the mixture. You'll find that it will triple in volume, then start to decrease in volume and thicken if you continue for too long.

To serve, place a portion of berries into your desired serving dish, then top with a generous spoon of the still-warm zabaglione.

Index

Grandma Olsen's ginger crunch